LITERATURE FROM CRESCENT MOON PUBLISHING

Rethinking Powys: Critical Essays on John Cowper Powys
edited by Jeremy Mark Robinson

The Ecstasies of John Cowper Powys
by A.P. Seabright

Postmodern Powys: New Essays on John Cowper Powys
by Joe Boulter

Thomas Hardy and John Cowper Powys: Wessex Revisited
by Jeremy Mark Robinson

Sexing Hardy: Thomas Hardy and Feminism
by Margaret Elvy

Thomas Hardy's Jude the Obscure: A Critical Study
by Margaret Elvy

Thomas Hardy's Tess of the d'Urbervilles: A Critical Study
by Margaret Elvy

Thomas Hardy: The Tragic Novels
by Tom Spenser

Stepping Forward: Essays, Lectures and Interviews
by Wolfgang Iser

Lawrence Durrell: Between Love and Death, Between East and West
by Jeremy Mark Robinson

Andrea Dworkin
by Jeremy Mark Robinson

German Romantic Poetry: Goethe, Novalis,
Heine, Hölderlin, Schlegel, Schiller
by Carol Appleby

Cavafy: Anatomy of a Soul
by Matt Crispin

Rilke: Space, Essence and Angels in the Poetry of Rainer Maria Rilke
by B.D. Barnacle

Dante: *Selections From the Vita Nuova*
translated by Thomas Okey

Friedrich Hölderlin: *Selected Poems*
translated by Michael Hamburger

Rainer Maria Rilke: *Selected Poems*
translated by Michael Hamburger

POSTMODERN POWYS

POSTMODERN POWYS

Essays On John Cowper Powys

Joe Boulter

CRESCENT MOON

Crescent Moon Publishing
P.O. Box 393
Maidstone
Kent
ME14 5XU, U.K.

First published 2000. Second edition 2008.
© Joe Boulter, 2000, 2008.

Printed and bound in Great Britain
Set in Book Antiqua 10 on 14pt.
This book is part of the John Cowper Powys Studies Series.

British Library Cataloguing in Publication data

Boulter, Joe
Postmodern Powys: Essays on John Cowper Powys
1. Powys, John Cowper, 1872-1963 – Criticism and interpretation
I. Title
823.9'12

ISBN 1-86171-166-1
ISBN-13 1861711663

Contents

Contents

Abbreviations

AN   *All or Nothing*. London: Macdonald, 1960.

LLW   *Letters of John Cowper Powys to Louis Wilkinson, 1935-53*. Ed. Louis Wilkinson. London: Macdonald, 1958.

LNR   *John Cowper Powys: Letters to Nicholas Ross*. Ed. Arthur Uphill. London: Bertram Rota, 1971.

OC   *Obstinate Cymric*. Carmarthen: Druid Press, 1947.

OG   *Owen Glendower: An Historical Novel*. 1940; London: The Bodley Head, 1941.

P   *Porius: A Romance of the Dark Ages*. 1951. Ed. Wilbur T. Albrecht. Hamilton: Colgate University Press, 1994.

W & S   *Wood and Stone: A Romance*. 1915; London: Heinemann, 1917.

WS   *Wolf Solent*. London: Jonathan Cape, 1929.

CCF   Stella Gibbons, *Cold Comfort Farm*, London: Longmans, Green and Co., 1932.

Introduction

METHOD OF INTERPRETATION

In these essays I do not argue that John Cowper Powys is a postmodernist novelist. Nor do I provide an interpretation of Powys using the techniques of postmodernist literary criticism. What I do is use some of the analogies between Powys's themes and techniques and the themes and techniques of postmodernist theorists as the basis for interpretations of some of Powys's novels. In other words, I do not interpret Powys as a postmodernist, or in a postmodernist way, I interpret him in the context of post-modernist theory.

I use this method of interpretation for two reasons. Firstly, as Fredric Jameson notes, postmodernism is the current cultural dominant.[1] If Powys is to be relevant today, he must be relevant in the context of postmodernist theory. Secondly, Powys and many postmodernist theorists have a common philosophical perspective. They are all, in a loose sense, pluralists. I explore this analogy in the first essay, 'What is the Saturnian Quest?' This common philosophical perspective leads to a shared interest in other issues, some of which I look at in essays on 'the other', 'performance' and 'parody'.

I hope that my interpretative approach will clarify how Powys's novels work and suggest ways in which they can be relevant today, as well as offering a fresh look at some of the problems with pluralism.

METHOD OF CITATION

References to Powys's works are given in the text, by abbreviation of the title and page number (the abbreviations are below). Where an essay focuses on a particular work, I omit the abbreviation of the title in the references to that work, as clarified in the endnotes. I have used the first UK editions of Powys's works except where a subsequent edition restores a large amount of text which was cut from the first edition in response to the publisher's demands (as is the case with *Porius*).

One

'The Saturnian Quest' in *Porius*

G. Wilson Knight says that the Saturnian Quest is one of the main themes of Powys's work, and that it is a quest for a Golden Age ruled by Cronos (Saturn).[1] He does not say what this Golden Age is. In this essay, I explore the meaning of the Saturnian Quest and the Golden Age in Powys's work through an interpretation of *Porius*. I focus on *Porius* because Powys thought it was his masterpiece (LLW 267 [18.6.49], LNR 101 [1.3.50]), and because Cronos appears in it, intending to institute a second Golden Age (872).[2]

My interpretation of *Porius* will show that the Saturnian Quest is a quest to institute a pluralist society. Pluralism (as I define it for the purpose of these essays) is the belief that being and knowledge do not exist independently. It is opposed to dualism, which (again, as I define it for the purpose of these essays) is the belief that being and knowledge do exist independently. For dualism what we know is true insofar as it corresponds to what is. For pluralism, truth is not determinable in this way: it is a label which we give to knowledge depending on our frame of reference.[3] *Porius* presents a conflict between pluralism and dualism, but this conflict is rigged. The arguments for a pluralist philosophy, a pluralist society, and a pluralist narrative technique take place within a pluralist philosophical framework, within a plural society and within a pluralist narrative. *Porius* can be read as a many-faceted discussion of the case for pluralism, and, as I will also show, many of the facets of Powys's arguments are analogous to the arguments for pluralism in postmodernist theory.

In *Porius*, the case for pluralism is focused on Myrddin Wyllt. Myrddin's pluralism is seen early on, when he tells Porius, '"I am what you see"' (60), indicating that his being depends on frames of reference. If Myrddin were what people saw, this would cause his identity to multiply by as many times as there were frames of reference to know him, and this is what happens in the novel. Powys names him in four different ways in chapter headings, as 'The Stranger', 'The Prophet', 'Myrddin Wyllt' and 'Cronos' (xxi-ii). Mabsant ap Kaw knows him by many different names (27), and he is said to act many different roles (60-61). For pluralism, what we know Myrddin as cannot be separated from what Myrddin *is*, and Powys describes Myrddin's acting as if this were the case, so that when he is acting as a 'prophet' we are told that he 'became, to Porius's fancy at least, a foot taller than Rhun', and when he is acting as an old woman, we are told that 'the prophet now became an old woman again' (61).

Powys's collapsing of the categories of being and knowing pre-figures the same collapse in postmodernist theory. Gilles Deleuze and Félix Guattari, for example, do not admit a distinction between representation and reality, and for Jean Baudrillard, in the current social state of 'simulation', there are no lies, only 'the facticity of facts'.[4] The link between Powys and postmodernist theory is William James's pragmatism. Powys acknowledged that James influenced him (A, 479), and this influence is clear in *Porius*: Porius's description of how his life illusion evolves, and Brother John's description of experimentation in values, are analogous to James's description of how opinions change (P, 31). Richard Rorty identifies similarities between James's pragmatism and postmodernist theory, and these similarities are illustrated by Deleuze and Guattari's work. Brian Massumi says that the question we should ask of *A Thousand Plateaus* is not 'is it true?' but 'does it work?'. For Deleuze, a concept is like a tool box, something to be used rather than tested for correspondence.[5]

James demonstrates pragmatist method by answering the question 'does the man go round the squirrel?' (P, 25) and what he demonstrates is that world versions are true only according to frames of reference, not by correspondence. The answer to the question is yes and no: it depends on your frame of reference. The different frames of reference could be produced by subjectivity: two people could visualise the tree, man and squirrel in different ways, or the word 'round' could be interpreted by two people in different ways. They could also be produced by deconstruction: 'round' is ambivalent in this context and whichever interpretation is chosen, the opposite interpretation is still present as a supplement.[6]

Postmodernist theory usually ignores the possibility of subjectivist pluralism, and argues for pluralism on the grounds that world versions are constructed by language.[7] There is, however, no pluralist reason for ignoring subjectivity. World versions could be plural if they did not exist beyond the frame of reference provided by language, but they could also be plural if they did not exist beyond the subject's frame of reference. The decision to opt for either language or subjectivity as the basis of pluralism is based on an *a priori* assumption: it cannot be argued effectively. When the idea that world versions are constructed by language makes its first appearance in twentieth-century theory, in Ferdinand de Saussure's *Course in General Linguistics*, it appears as an *a priori* assumption.[8]

Michel Foucault says that 'mental illness' is constituted by 'statements'. This nominalism is based on Saussure's assumption that world versions are constructed by language. Nominalism leads to pluralism when Foucault says that Borges's fictional worlds can be heterotopic because they are discursive.[9] This implies that the world can be heterotopic because it too is discursive, constructed by different statements which can say incommensurable things. Deconstruction is also based on Saussure's assumption,[10] but Jacques Derrida's argument is rather that the same statements can have incommensurable inter-pretations. So, for example, Derrida offers a reinterpretation of Descartes's hypothesis of the malicious demon, in which he argues that Descartes does not say that the subject might be wrong, that what he says is that the language-constructed world can be interpreted in two incommensurable ways: it includes both madness and reason.[11] The move from different statements to different interpretations is useful politically, since even if the world is constructed by commensurable statements, it can be interpreted in incommensurable ways.

Deconstruction, then, has two stages. Firstly, it accepts Saussure's assumption that language constructs world versions rather than corresponding to a world. Secondly, it argues that this means that the significance of any statement cannot be reduced to a single interpretation, since the principle of any such reduction would be that the interpretation in question identified the referents of the statement, and according to Saussure's assumption, statements do not have referents. When Baudrillard argues that the use value of objects is a form of exchange value, and when he compares his collapse of use value into exchange value to deconstruction's collapse of denotation into connotation, he provides a theory of goods which is analogous to stage one of deconstruction.[12] Surprisingly, Baudrillard does not get to stage two: he does not see his collapse of use value into exchange value as an enabling device which will allow the significance of goods to become plural. This, though, is exactly what Michel de Certeau does see.[13] Certeau also compares consumption to the collapse of denotation into connotation, but he sees this as leading to consumption which is itself a form of production, or 'resignific-ation', the equivalent of a writerly approach to a readerly text in which the intended interpretation of the goods is treated as just one among a plurality of possible and equally valid inter-pretations.[14]

Instead of suggesting that the state of simulation allows for a reinterpretation of goods by consumers, Baudrillard privileges the pre-modern model of consumption he calls 'symbolic exchange'. In symbolic exchange, the exchanged object has very similar characteristics to Certeau's consumed object. Above all, it is ambivalent. It is surprising that Baudrillard does not see the analogy between symbolic exchange and simulation, since he says himself that the 'symbolic obligation' is the abolition of value and that in the 'fractal' stage of simulation things are freed from their values. Why should the loss of value result in ambivalence for symbolic exchange but not for simulation?[15]

Deleuze and Guattari are unusual in postmodern theory, because they recognise both subjective and deconstructive pluralism. They see both subjectivity and deconstruction as ways of achieving partial deterritorialisation. The deterritorialisations are partial, since they are premissed on either one of subjectivity and deconstruction being true and the other being false. For Deleuze and Guattari the only really deterritorialised state, 'positive absolute deterritorialisation on the plane of consistency', is the one in which body, mind and language are placed on the same plane, and the dualist idea of correspondence between the categories is abandoned.[16] In this, Deleuze and Guattari differ from Foucault, who privileges the sixteenth-century episteme for collapsing representation and reality into 'one vast text', from Baudrillard, who says that trying to get beyond appearances is an illusion and is wrong, and from deconstruction, which they think is 'still the domain of representation'.[17]

Deleuze and Guattari's collapse of the basic categories of epistemological dualism (object, subject, representation) is analogous to James's argument that there is 'only one primal stuff or material in our world' and that object and subject are the terms of a relation between one part of that experience and another part, the relation itself being knowledge.[18] It is a collapse which occurs frequently in Powys, who tells us, for example, that 'Porius had been mixing this tree with several of his recent thoughts' (28).

This is the pluralist world version, the world version for which postmodernist theory, William James and *Porius* all argue, in their different ways. The problem which pluralists encounter in arguing for pluralism is that if you are trying to persuade someone that your world version is best, you tend eventually to base your argument on the correspondence of knowledge to being, and that correspondence is the very thing which pluralism denies. Deleuze and Guattari, for example, say that books do not correspond to anything outside themselves, but at the same time they continually imply that their book does correspond to how things really are. They criticise dialectical thought on the grounds that nature does not work dialectically. They make frequent analogies between their own philosophical term 'deterritorial-isation' and such natural phenomena as rhizomes and nomadism, implying that deterritorialisation is natural. Similarly, Foucault can only account for epistemic shifts by calling them 'autochthonous', just as James can only account for change by appeal to 'new experience'.[19] The appeal to nature also occurs in *Porius*, where Myrddin hears the coming of the second Golden

Age as a prophesy of the earth (320).

These appeals to nature occur in arguments for pluralism, though they are contrary to pluralism, because it is very difficult to argue in any other way. As Stanley Fish says, belief in the constructed nature of fact does not alter our belief in facts not presently being shown to be constructions, and not all constructions can be challenged at the same time. A pluralist believes in the constructed nature of fact, but this does not alter his belief that 'the constructed nature of fact' is a fact, since *this* construction cannot be challenged if all the other constructions are to be challenged. It is easy to slip from believing in the fact that 'fact is constructed' to believing that the fact that 'fact is constructed' is the one fact which is not constructed. Baudrillard slips in this way when he says things like, 'we have flown free of the referential sphere of the real and of history'.[20]

To prevent this slip into paradox, pluralism must ensure that the constructed facts which it does not challenge are not presented as corresponding to how things really are. In Gianni Vattimo's terms, it must avoid installing hermeneutics (which is the philosophy that there are no facts, only interpretations) as a metaphysics (as fact), since hermeneutics is an interpretation too. The slip is avoided when hermeneutics is presented as an interpretation, which means being presented as a 'fable' or 'myth'.[21]

Vattimo illustrates what hermeneutics is with the example of Nietzsche's announcement of the death of God, which, he says, was truly an announcement. Nietzsche does not show that 'God' does not correspond to absolute reality. He shifts the frame of reference which used to construct God, so that it no longer constructs God. Vattimo also uses 'the death of God' as a metaphor for the inauguration of the era of hermeneutics. In this metaphor, God is a figure for absolute reality, and his death means a shift from belief in correspondence to belief in hermeneutics as the dominant fable. In this way Vattimo is consistently hermeneutic in his defence of hermeneutics. He tells the story of the inauguration of the hermeneutic era not as a discovery that correspondence does not exist, but as the construction of a set of beliefs under which correspondence does not exist. He also tells the story in a way which emphasises that process of construction by telling it as a story, using a metaphor, the death of God.[22]

Powys uses the same metaphor to tell the same story. In *Porius*, Myrddin tells Neb that (as Cronos) he unmade himself (divested himself of his godhood) to inaugurate the first Golden Age and will unmake himself to inaugurate the second Golden Age (286-7). This unmaking will perform two functions. Firstly, it will shift belief away from correspondence and towards pluralism by removing the possibility of an absolute reality for facts to correspond to (as in Vattimo, God is a figure for absolute reality). Secondly, since the absolute reality which Cronos would stand for is (paradoxically) pluralist absolute reality, it will prevent the shift to pluralism becoming a slip from one absolute to another.

Myrddin says that he will unmake himself as Cronos, but this unmaking in the future is prefigured by his deauthorisation in the present. This is one instance of Powys rigging the case for pluralism in *Porius* so that the future Golden Age is anticipated in Edeyrnion by the pluralism already present there. Myrddin is deauthorised firstly by being subject to attacks of physical frailty (62). Powys says that he may not really be frail, he may be acting frail (64, 75). This leads us to two conclusions, firstly that Myrddin's deauthorisation may be voluntary (which is consistent with his wish to unmake himself as Cronos), secondly that in Myrddin the distinction between being and knowing is collapsed, he is what he appears to be. Powys says, in fact, that his 'reduction' is the same, whether of not it is real or acted (65).

Myrddin also attempts to deauthorise himself by persuading the Henog to record that Nineue had power over Myrddin. Neb says that he does this '"Because as long as the Three-in-One rules in Heaven, cruelty and love and lies rule on earth"' (283). Neb's implication is that Myrddin must deauthorise himself in order to prevent the Saturnian era being the same as the Christian era, to prevent it being an era in which Cronos is installed as an absolute. One instance of this avoidance of authority is the fact that it is Neb rather than Myrddin who indicates that Myrddin is Cronos (285). At the one point where Myrddin does make assertions about his role as Cronos, which is the point where he explains that he will institute pluralism on earth by unmaking himself as a god, he immediately catches himself up, saying '"A fine example I'm showing... of 'crooked-counselling'! Aye I know it! The whole thing, all my half-memories, all my supervisions, may be pure imagination."' (287). By 'crooked-counselling', Myrddin means the advancement of arguments in a deauthorised way, as provisionals, and he proceeds immediately to provisionalise his own account of his strategy of deauthorisation (a fine example of consistency) by saying it may all be his imagination (he does so again at p. 294). He goes on to approve of Neb's opinion that obedience is a bad thing, on the grounds that what turns a god into a devil is power (287). Even Myrddin's physical characteristics are consistent with pluralist deauthorisation. As his huge ears imply, he is open to other people's points of view: the first thing Rhun does when he meets him is tell him what he has been doing (56-57). On the other hand, he is not an effective speaker, his tone of voice hinders people from listening to him (100).

Myrddin's failure to install himself as an absolute illustrates the difference between 'Saturnalian' and 'Saturnian'. Under dualism, Myrddin is Saturnalian, since he is the figure for an inversion of the dominant social or interpretative order. For the dualists in *Porius* he is a Satanic figure. Rhun calls Neb an 'imp of Satan' (309, repeated by Powys 317); Gorsant says that Myrddin is '"invoking Beelzebub"' (316); calls him 'Satan's dung', and encourages the Christians to ride their horses over him (501); and the Derwydd accuses him of corrupting the emperor with the help of Satan (317). Under pluralism, as we have seen, Myrddin is not Satanic but Saturnian. He does not want to overthrow God and install himself in God's place, he wants to unmake the category of godhood.

The distinction between Saturnalian and Saturnian is a distinction between inversion and dehierarchisation. According to Neb, in the Saturnalia all the masters become slaves and all the slaves become masters, 'in anticipation' of the Golden Age (285). The inversion of hierarchy in Saturnalia anticipates the abolition of hierarchy in the Saturnian Age, but it is not itself an abolition of hierarchy. Yssylt wants to turn the Feast of the Sowing from a Saturnalia to a revolutionary overthrow of the Brythons, from a figural to a literal inversion, but this would still mean an inversion, not a dehierarchisation (476).

Postmodernist theory also recognises that while Saturnalia – or 'carnival' – inverts the dominant order, it preserves the hierarchical organisation on which that order is based. Juliet Mitchell says carnival 'disrupts only within the terms of...[the] law'; Baudrillard criticises Marxism on the grounds that its opposition to capitalism is founded on sharing the same absolutes as capitalism: both find the 'real' in labour and production. For Baudrillard, Marxism is Saturnalian. Postmodernist theory, like Myrddin, attempts to be Saturnian: Robert Young introduces the poststructuralist project as the search for an alternative to the Hegelian dialectic, as the attempt to dehierarchise without inverting (and so repeating) the existing hierarchy.[23]

In both postmodernist theory and Powys there is an explicit link between resistance to the Hegelian dialectic and resistance to political absolutism. Deleuze and Guattari are explicitly anti-Hegelian and implicitly non-fascist.[24] Powys tells Louis Wilkinson that Hitler's world is Hegelian and ours is pluralistic (86 LLW, 12.12.40). In *Porius*, Myrddin's pluralism is implicitly non-Nazi: As Porius frees him from y Wyddfa, eagles begin to scream. The eagles are described firstly as Myrddin's enemies, secondly as the friends of tyrants, and thirdly as 'Birds of Absolute Power' (871-2).

For Porius, Myrddin and Christianity are opposites (66), and in *Porius*, Christianity stands in for Nazism as the dominant form of absolutism (734). Christian absolutism is seen to be founded on a belief that our knowledge is true insofar as it corresponds to God's knowledge, as the Derwydd indicates by saying that his interpretations fall short of 'the divine truth' (317). Porius rejects this Platonic version of Christianity by saying, '"If such are God's thoughts... they are certainly very different from mine!"' (639). Because it is founded on correspondence, Christianity inverts any orders it challenges, rather than dehierarchising them. Powys says that it commands people to 'adore what they had been burning, and to burn what they had been adoring' (xvii). Atheism, however, is also founded on correspondence, and is to Christianity what Marxism is to capitalism. In *Porius*, Morvran's hostility to Christianity is a furious, one-sided revolt which is as absolutist as Christianity itself. The pluralist attitude to Christianity is Porius's 'suspension of judgement' (485).

In Edeyrnion, the old gods are 'departing' and the new Christian God has arrived (xvii-xix). When Brochvael imagines Gorsant building up the walls of his church and shutting out the natural world (166), the implication is that the Christian world version will be unnaturally limiting. In the present of the novel, however, the limitation has not yet happened. *Porius* is pluralist to the extent that even Christianity has its pluralist version, Pelagianism (42, 152, 399-400), and the god who 'triumphs' – after his pluralist fashion – is an old one: Cronos. When Gorsant launches his attack on Myrddin, no one pays any attention to him, and he dies immediately afterwards (504). The concluding chapter of the novel is called 'Cronos', indicating that Myrddin is Cronos, and is focused on Myrddin's evasion of imprisonment by Nineue (826-873), indicating that he will be able to inaugurate the second Golden Age.

Though, in *Porius*, the Saturnian Age will be inaugurated at some point in the future, Porius himself achieves his Saturnian Quest. Inspired by Pelagianism (40), he casts off the 'false conscience' of Christianity and social duty from the 'free pulses of his life' (37). He has what Deleuze and Guattari privilege as experiences in which we can see 'the light begin to break through the cracks in our all too closed minds'.[25] He is 'a man for whom an authentic crack had yawned in the familiar system of things, *letting something else show through*' (631), and what he sees is existence 'as *many worlds*' (632). This experience leads him to conclude that 'truth' is determined by frame of reference (592), and he argues for subjectivist pluralism in his conversation with Medrawd (851-2).

Though Porius's development is presented as a conversion to pluralism, he begins the novel as a theoretical and a practical pluralist. On the first day his sense of liberation and exaltation comes from his idea that individual subjects can create their own futures by the power of imagination (42, 48, 53). In practical terms, he is a pluralist too. He finds it difficult to make decisions (14. He cannot decide, for example, whether he finds the smell of the Cewri alluring or revolting ([534]). This is because he sees both sides of issues: he can look from the watch-tower in different directions, and this makes him seem like different men (15), he is able to make mental journeys in various directions (78), and he is a man who can say 'Jesus Christ' (14) while having something in his blood which is 'un-Aryanized and unchristianized' (13). He also collapses the physical and the mental after the fashion of Deleuze and Guattari, James, and Powys himself: he sees every mental situation as a physical sensation (33, 657).

Porius's pluralism should not be seen as a subversion of the dominant order in Edeyrnion, since Einion is pluralist too. For both father and son, attachment to an absolute, like Mithras or Christ, is just a game (45). Einion is a humorous sceptic who has one dominant passion, the superstitions of the forest-people (8). His passion for these superstitions is due to their subversiveness. As a pluralist, he naturally supports the world version which subverts standard ways of thinking. Like Porius he is also reluctant to take decisions (216).

In *Obstinate Cymric* Powys credits the Welsh with memories of a Saturnian Golden Age (OC, 83), and with a pluralist philosophy (OC 7). In *Porius* the characters are consistent with this construction of Welsh identity: as well as Einion and Porius, many other characters are pluralist. Brochvael, for example, admires Hadrian because he is sceptical and tolerant, believing in nothing and everything (268). Meanwhile, the anti-pluralist characters have their dualism challenged by pluralist experiences. Like Porius, Euronwy experiences one of those cracks in the system of things in which more than one version of the world is seen at the same time (787-8).

The comparison of Powys with Deleuze and Guattari showed that pluralism can have a political purpose: the Saturnian Quest is not just for a pluralist state of mind, but for a plural society. In *Porius* Brochvael's servant Gwrgi is a social pluralist, since he does not want to rule (162-3). Gwrgi characterises the Romans, the Brythons and the Saxons as all participating in the same hierarchical way of thinking: they all strive to conquer one another. He characterises the forest-people's lack of interest in conquering by referring to the fact that he does not use iron in the goad he uses for his horse. He sees rule as no more than putting a name on the land. Ruling does not establish the ruler as right, or true, and the succession of conquerors in Edeyrnion illustrates this. The forest-people have existed alongside the various conquerors without ever accepting, or rejecting (which is still an acknowledgement of hierarchisation) their rule as anything other than a name.

Like Baudrillard's masses, the forest-people resist or refuse the ultimate meaning of the absolutes with which they are confronted. They ignore the conquerors: the eyebrows of their Derwydd seem to express 'an innocent mockery of all the established reputations, human or divine, from the beginning of the world' (260), and the Derwydd treats the whole of human life as if it were just a titillatingly thrilling story (262). The forest-people have the same figural role in *Porius* as the weed has in *A Thousand Plateaus*. Deleuze and Guattari describe the weed (using Henry Miller) as 'a state of China', 'the Dark Age', the thing which fills the places left by cultivated areas and eventually gets the upper hand.[26] Neither the forest-people nor the weed need be deterritorialised, because neither has ever been territorialised to begin with. Both are figures for the same non-participatory, non-hierarchical, pluralist strategy. This nonparticipation in the conquer-and-rule frame of reference is experienced by one conqueror, the Roman Aulus, as a lack in the forest-people: he says they have '"no laws… no customs, no traditions!"' (212). But they do have traditions, just different ones. Powys says that 'their whole way of life was non-Aryan and non-Celtic. It was communistic and matriarchal' (8, 321-2). Since it is communistic and matriarchal, the forest-people's society could be seen as an inversion of Brythonic society, rather than as a dehierarchisation. Powys encourages this interpretation by referring to the problems caused for Erddud by the conversion of the 'custom' of matriarchy into 'absolute law' (326). This conversion illustrates the tendency for the forest-people's Saturnianism to slip into Saturnalianism, but just as Saturnalia can be seen as anticipating the Golden Age, so the forest-people's inversion of the Brythonic hierarchy could be seen as a figure for dehierarchisation. Einion sees the forest-people in this way when he says that they have never had their Golden Age (he does not mean a Saturnian Age in this context, but an age of conquest and rule) and that they 'don't want it anyway' which is why they cannot really be conquered (207, Brochvael agrees, 223, 247).

The pluralism of the forest-people corresponds to a pluralist social reality in Edeyrnion. The region is populated by great mixture of ethnic groups, and it is unclear who the original inhabitants were (3-4, 124, 143); in other words, the forest-people are right to regard conquerors as putting no more than a new name on the land. The history of ethnic change in Britain as it is accepted in *Porius* also mingles fact and fiction, including giants, 'Coranians' and people from Atlantis as well as Picts, Goidels, Brythons and Romans (3-4). The ethnic groups which co-exist in Edeyrnion are incommensurable not just because the ethnic groups have different beliefs, but because some of the ethnic groups, from our frame of reference, occupy different orders of being.

This ethnic mixedness leads to a molecularity to the Edeyrnion society which undermines the molar oppositions of Brython and Saxon.[27] This molecularity is not just a question of there being more opposed groups than Saxon and Brython (this would just be more molarity), but of there being people who fit into more than one category, of whom the most prominent is Porius himself. Porius is part-Brython, part-Roman, part-Cewri and part-forest-people (4, 8, 55). Consequently although his official role is heir to the Prince of Edeyrnion, his sympathy is with the forest-people, the Cewri and the Ffichti (153-4). Powys indicates that this ethnic mixing will continue after the Saxon conquest: he shows this figurally when Arthur's blood mixes with the blood of the Saxon he has killed, and literally in Gunta, the child of Sibylla the Gwyddyl-Ffichti girl and Gunhorst the Saxon (xxii).

Porius has what Deleuze and Guattari call a schizo-identity

(*Plateaus*, 29-33). He is the son of the reigning Prince of Edeyrnion, he is very strong (so he is a hero), but he is short, and he spends the first eighteen pages of the novel standing still while engaged in a rambling series of speculations (so he is not a hero). His personal life has nothing to do with his role as a Brythonic Prince and is based on his Cewri descent (137). Porius himself is aware of this discrepancy within his identity: returning from his personal adventure with the Cewri, he recognises that he has deserted the Brython struggle against the Saxons, and says to himself '"I surely am the least heroic and most unpatriotic offspring of a Brythonic chieftain ever born!"' (556). Powys reinforces this impression when he shows Porius falling asleep 'with a Sais-child leaning against him, his father and grandfather wounded to death, his mother seduced, his bride in love with his friend, and himself the clumsy murderer [of the Cawres]' (628).

Porius subverts traditional social categories in *Porius* b y belonging to several groups at the same time. Another form of subversion occurs when the members of opposed groups join the same new group. One such new group is the 'Cymry' (372, see also 543). The Cymry, or the ordinary people of Wales, are still formed according to hierarchical rules, but theirs is a functional opposition rather than an immanent one: they are opposed to power, rather than particular groups in power. Gwythyr illustrates this functional conception of identity by saying '"We were all foreigners once!"' (372). The Cymry offer a pragmatist account of group identity which could be extended to all groups. It is only, for example, in one interpretation that Porius is Brythonic and Morfydd is Brythonic. Matrilinearity would say that they are respectively Roman and Gwyddyl-Ffichti. A further dehierarch-isation occurs when, by making himself the object of Gwythyr and Mabsant's ridicule, Lot-el-Azziz shows how the opposition between Cymry and rulers can be overcome by a functional union of members of both groups in opposition to a third party

(Lot himself) (375-8). The Cymry themselves shift from idea to reality when under Myrddin's enchantment the conflicting sides in the riot at the Feast of the Sowing begin to fraternise. Myrddin names the fraternisation 'Cymry' (507-8).

Consequently, although the Cymry are oppositional in approach, their oppositionality leads to a general sense of the deconstruction of oppositions since their opposition leads us to see that all oppositions are produced by frames of reference. This kind of political tactic can be seen at work in the various kinds of inversion in *Porius*, which imply dehierarchisation. The most obvious inversion (after the presentation of Christianity as a figure for Nazism) occurs in the presentation of Arthur. Arthur's court is seen by Porius as an uncivilising influence which might turn him into a savage (95), and Galahaut is presented by Powys as a lecherous coward (768). Powys also illustrates that the standard Galahad is the product of narrative, not a reality, by showing Cretinloy transforming his '"most cowardly retreats into heroic deeds and [...] most lecherous obsessions into emotions of piety and purity"' (769).

Porius also inverts our preconceptions about social power. Although the Brythonic men are the representatives of power, they are not particularly interested in it, they are more interested in philosophy and sex. Porius is interested in Myrddin and the Cewri, Einion is interested in the forest-people's superstitions, hunting and light-loves (9), and Brochvael is interested in books, Sibylla and Drom (460, 612-13). Power is wielded by the Brythonic women. Einion returns to the Gaer having broken the sword of Cunedda, 'smiling just the same'. It is Morfydd who sees him as an 'idiotic fool', and who identifies the sword's traditional meaning as 'the House of Cunedda's lasting dominion over Edeyrnion' (205). Similarly, it is Morfydd and Euronwy who decide on Morfydd's marriage to Porius (216-7).

Einion is responsible for the most blatant misuse of a sign of power in *Porius*: he plunges the sword of Cunedda into the ground 'As unceremoniously as if it had been a spade or a pitchfork'. He does so because it has a purely personal 'special and peculiar pleasure' for him, perhaps a pleasure derived from seeing how deeply he can push it in. In doing so, he breaks off the end (145-6). Einion's action is a pluralist one. He takes a sign which has a lot of traditional meaning invested in it (for example, Brythonic rule, Brythonic succession, and the patriarchy) and gives it his own supplementary meaning. In doing so, he shows the multivalent significance of the sword as a sign, and undercuts the traditional meanings. This undercutting would take place without the sword being broken: the fact that it is broken simply reinforces the idea that the multivalence of its significance has been revealed.

Einion's misuse of the sword of Cunedda is analogous to Certeau's resignification, and Baudrillard's symbolic exchange. Throughout *Porius*, objects are exchanged and misused in the same way. On the first page of the novel, for example, we learn that Porius is to go to Saint Julian's Fountain to fetch a pitcher of holy water for Porius Manlius (3). When Rhun arrives on the watch-tower, he gives Porius Porius Manlius's water flask, which is always used for this purpose (19). Later on, Porius Manlius tells Aulus that he hopes Porius has not forgotten to fill the flask (211). Still later, Porius himself finds the flask lying empty on the ground in front of his bridal tent. While Porius has clearly been deflected from the proper or intended use of the flask, he has also given it his own meaning: 'it had come to be endowed for him with a sort of symbolic significance' (556), so that when he picks up the flask he uses it as part of a private superstition to push some twigs into a perfect square (557). It is not only objects but spaces which are shown to have different uses (and therefore from a pragmatist point of view different meanings). Brother John's cell is a religious space and a living space, but is also used for storytelling and childbirth (574).

The storyteller in Brother John's cell is the Henog. The Henog's attitude to narrative illustrates the potential for pluralism to slip into a paradoxical assertion of its own correspondence to how things really are. When the Henog first appears he is a dualist. His first words are a criticism of imprecision, of mist, of being lost, of the 'Cimmerian' nature of the mist,[28] and an assertion of the need to find the way and to tell the truth (84). He places great importance on what has happened, rather than on what might happen (89) presumably because it is easier to believe in past events as facts. He stresses that events follow one another 'naturally' and 'surely' and believes that some events can be called 'real' (90). Later, though, he seems pluralist, saying that he does not sift fact from fable, because '"in reality"' fables can be more '"revealing of nature's secrets"' than fact (440). Later still he seems even more explicitly pluralist, asking who, if he says that 'the ultimate reality' is 'the Many', can judge whether he is right or wrong (806-7). In both these cases though, the Henog's pluralism slips back into dualism, since he argues for pluralism on the basis of correspondence to absolute reality.

The Henog's ultimately dualist desire to say what reality is is thwarted in several ways. When Gwendydd asks Neb what he thinks *will* happen, the Henog asks Neb to stop and to tell him again what *has* happened in the correct order (96-97). Neb responds by lying. The Henog's own style of narration is anti-pluralist in that it does not accommodate interruptions and questions (91). As a result his narrative is so limited that it lulls Porius to sleep (91-92). This in turn shows that facts are facts only for those who know them.

The factual approach to narrative is also undercut by the fact that Porius thinks of the Henog's narrative as an art: his factuality is achieved by 'technique', it does not consist in the discovery of facts (92). This is borne out by the fact that despite his initial emphasis on facts, he is seen to be more concerned with their representation, even down to the formation of letters (104), and by the fact that when Powys describes how the Henog would have translated Porius's experience into narrative, he says that his interpretation of Porius's motives would have been 'wholly wrong' (547, see also 715).

In contrast to the Henog, Myrddin maintains that the truth is not available, and he invites the Henog to imagine how irrelevant his history will be to future generations (102-3). His implication is that statements are not valuable because they correspond to an absolute reality and are therefore true. Instead, they are valuable inasmuch as they are useful, from a particular frame of reference. Later in the novel, Porius treats history in just this way, altering his opinion of the truth of Medrawd's claim to have slept with Euronwy when it suits him to do so (624-5).

Myrddin encourages us to take a pragmatist attitude towards narrative, and he also encourages us to take a pragmatist attitude towards his own narratives, by deauthorising himself. He deauthorises himself, for example, when he makes his prophesy about the future of Britain (which is an accurate metaphorical description of British history until the Second World War). He relies on Porius to hold him up while he speaks, and he stops short in the middle of a sentence, gasping (106-7). Porius finds his speech comical (107), but at the same time he feels that it has some force (107-8). Myrddin's deauthorisation of his own prophesy is not in conflict with his intention, since he begins by saying that '"why should anybody understand me? *It were wiser not to!*"' (106). It would be wiser not to understand Myrddin because to understand him would be to adopt his frame of reference, rather than maintaining our own. This would be contrary to pluralism. Myrddin does not want anyone to believe him, in the sense of believing that what he says corresponds to absolute reality.

Myrddin's prophesies are stories which aspire to a very

different kind of reader response from the Henog's histories. Firstly because they are stories about the future, but secondly because they are told in a way which deauthorises the teller. The world version of Myrddin's prophecies is factitious, and its facticity is what enables it to be heterotopic. Myrddin says that he contains a plurality of futures present within him, and Porius asks '"How can there possibly be more than one?"' (125-6). The answer is in the question: the future is plural because it is present as possibility, rather than as absolute reality. It is shown to be possibility rather than absolute reality because Myrddin is deauthorised: at the same time as Porius experiences the 'impressions of multiplicity' to which Myrddin provides access, he is holding Myrddin up, just as he will do when Myrddin makes his prophesy (65, 106-7).

Powys saw Myrddin as a representation of himself (LLW 286 [9.1.52]), and Powys's novel has the same factitious quality as Myrddin's stories. As with Myrddin, the facticity prevents the slip into an assertion of pluralism as how things really are, since it invites a reader response which views the pluralist world version of *Porius* not as how things really are, but as how things could be.

Powys invites this kind of response by making us aware that his story constructs rather than describes a world version. One way in which he does this is to frustrate our expectations. For example, on page five we learn that Porius has two important pieces of news, but it is not until page 32 that we find out what this news is (he will marry Morfydd and join Arthur's campaign against the Saxon). Even at the point of telling, the news is delayed by the insertion of a series of short descriptions of Porius waiting for Rhun's response, and inviting him to guess what the news is (31-32). When it is finally told, the second piece of news is not told directly at all but reported by Powys, who says, as if to satirise the extent to which he has prevaricated, that Porius told Rhun 'bluntly' (32). The world version of *Porius* is constructed by a collaboration between Powys (who offers the reader things to make-believe in) and the reader (who make-believes in them). By making the collaboration difficult, Powys alerts the reader to the process of construction.

Powys alerts us to the process of construction in many different ways. As well as the order in which he narrates, he uses the style in which he narrates as a means of making the collaboration difficult. When he says 'The air of this late autumn afternoon was as full of softly-drifting, lightly-undulating waves of terrestrial coolness as it was open over their heads to the motionless spaces of the untroubled sky' (23), 'as it was' invites a redundant comparison. Its only effect is to alert us to the fact that Powys is making up the story. Powys achieves this effect with many other stylistic techniques, including unexpected diction such as academic note style (34, 69), and archaisms (for example, 'ere' ([29]), using 'abode' as a verb [15]).

By marking their stories as factitious, Powys and Myrddin maintain consistency by arguing for pluralism in a pluralist way. Some postmodernist theorists do the same. Baudrillard writes in a 'poetic style'. Deleuze and Guattari try to neutralise the effects of power from their own discourse by deauthorising themselves through humour, and advertising the literariness of their own style. They describe the process of writing *A Thousand Plateaus* flippantly, making us take what they have written less seriously. The most sustained example of their self-deauthorisation is in chapter three of *A Thousand Plateaus*, which is written as the report of a lecture by Arthur Conan Doyle's Professor Challenger. The lecture is deauthorised in many ways. Like much of *A Thousand Plateaus* it contains odd statements such as 'God is a Lobster'. Challenger's audience leaves, indicating that his lecture (and thus Deleuze and Guattari's point) is not worth listening to. His authority is disputed. He is incoherent, as a being: he has, like Deleuze and Guattari themselves, a plural identity. The chapter itself mixes fictional characters such as Challenger with real characters such as Hjelmslev, as well as realistic events such as the giving of a lecture with marvellous events such as Challenger turning into different animals and disintegrating. This indicates that the world version of *A Thousand Plateaus* is heterotopic, and does not correspond to an absolute reality.[29]

Powys also creates a sense of facticity by including real and fictional characters and realistic and marvellous events in the *Porius* world version. Real characters such as Pelagius, realistic but fictional characters such as Aulus, legendary characters such as Arthur, and mythical characters such as Blodeuwedd, are all to be found in Edeyrnion. Powys can be highly realistic in his attention to physical details, telling us that Porius 'pressed the front of his wrists against the high coping of the wide stone battlement' (5), but he also reports the marvellous as if it were fact, saying, for example, that 'the thoughts of the Derwydd had the power of moving from brain to brain' (309).

Deleuze and Guattari's, and Powys's, facticity is consistent with the pluralist argument that it is not possible to make distinctions between fact and fiction, since facts are only facts inasmuch as you believe in them (factuality is given to things rather than immanent in them; even the distinction I make between the realistic and the marvellous is based on a traditional frame of reference rather than on the events in *A Thousand Plateaus* or *Porius* actually being real or marvellous). One of the consequences of this argument is that things will turn out to be facts if you believe that they will: frame of reference determines what kind of world version we experience. Baudrillard calls this the precession of the simulacrum.[30] Porius believes in the precession of the simulacrum, though from a subjectivist perspective: he believes that he can create the future through his imagination (42, 49). Once again, pluralist theory is realised in *Porius*, as Porius's wishes are fulfilled: he dreams of sex with a Cawres (536-7) and the dream is realised (547).

The way Powys focalises events in *Porius* is also consistent with pluralism. Powys's focalisation is rhizomatic, in that it does not allow itself to be overcoded with a particular hierarchy of events,[31] it continually shifts our attention from what we would categorise as the sublime to what we would categorise as the ridiculous. As Einion is dying, he farts (645). When Porius, Rhun and Rhun's dog Drudwyn enter Gwendydd and Nineue's pavilion, each, including the dog, is given a three line paragraph describing their reaction (74). Later, the pavilion itself is invaded by a cow and a horse, and the horse shits, much to the gratific-ation of Porius's pluralist sensibility (119). Porius anticipates the trajectory of the novel as a whole at this point by describing himself and Rhun as '"soldiers of Mithras turned into herdsmen of Myrddin"' (120).

We are continually unsettled while reading *Porius*, both by what Powys chooses to show us of what happens, and by what happens itself. After unexpectedly beginning his novel with eighteen pages during which Porius stands still, he then describes Porius and Rhun setting off on a run which takes them in unexpected directions, so that Porius thinks to himself, 'where in the name of Jesus was he off to now?' (19, 21). As readers, we might well continue to think the same thing throughout the novel. Powys's focalisation and his plot are continually digressing, to the extent that there is no way to distinguish between what is digression and what is not.[32] In reading *Porius*, we take the kind of 'stroll' that is so important to Deleuze and Guattari, a journey of continual deterritorialisation in which all the categories we bring to the novel, and all the categories the novel constructs, are shown to be constructions.[33]

At the end of *Porius*, Powys might well say, along with Porius, '"There are many gods; and I have served a great one"' (873). Powys has followed a Saturnian Quest: *Porius* is a multi-faceted argument for pluralism. He has also followed it in a Saturnian way: the novel is also a consistent argument for pluralism. It shows us that there are only interpretations, and it shows us that what it shows us is only an interpretation.

Two

Porius, Pluralism and Powys's 'Weak Sense of the "Other"'

In the last sentence of *Porius,* Porius says that he must tell Morfydd about his experience with Myrddin, because '"she alone will understand"' (873).[1] According to dualism, it is possible for Morfydd to know what Porius is talking about, since when he tells her about his experience, what he says will correspond to a lesser or a greater extent to a reality which it is possible for them both to know. According to pluralism, though, it is not possible for Morfydd to know what Porius is talking about, since what she knows is her world version, what he knows is his, and world versions do not correspond to a reality beyond themselves. In this essay I will explore how Powys responds to this problem for pluralism in *Porius.*

The problem of not being able to have a dialogue between world versions is discussed in postmodernist theory as the problem of the 'other'. The most consistently pluralist approach to the problem of the other is the one which simply gives up, and says that if the other really is other (if Porius really does have a different world version to Morfydd) then there is nothing to say. There have been other approaches which have attempted to provide for dialogue, in other words, which have attempted to explain how it is possible to have a relation with the other as other, but these have been implicitly dualist. Young provides one example of this implicit dualism when he refers to 'The appropriation of the other as a form of knowledge within a totalising system'.[2] 'Appropriation' is an ambiguous word to use, but it expresses a common idea in postmodernist theory. It implies that when I experience the other as a form of knowledge within a totalising system, I take possession of it without authority. I experience it, but I do not experience it properly. It also implies that it is possible for me to experience the other without experiencing it as a form of knowledge within a totalising system, in a way which would enable me to experience it properly. This implication rests on the dualist assumption that my experience of the other can be tested for correspondence to the other itself, to establish if it is proper.

Young's argument is attractive because he refers to a 'totalising system'. We are likely to say to ourselves that while totalising systems like 'the Media' appropriate the other, we know the other as other on a personal level. As experiences of French culture the TV documentary I watch about France might seem improper whereas my own visit to France might seem proper. Pluralism, however, does not allow us to make this distinction between theoretical and personal relations, since the world versions in pluralism are produced by the subject or by discourse. If there is such a thing as subjectivity, I cannot have experience not-as-a-subject. If Saussure's assumption is right, I cannot have experience not-categorised-by-language. In the same way, though

Heidegger's 'comprehension' involves the whole person, rather than a theoretical attitude, comprehension continues to appropriate the other. For Emmanuel Levinas, 'To comprehend is to be related to the particular that exists only through knowledge, which is always knowledge of the universal.'[3]

Levinas's own argument for the possibility of dialogue posits a relation to the other which is presupposed by comprehension. Levinas argues that if we think of language not as subordinate to the consciousness we have of the presence of the other, but as the condition of any conscious grasp, we recognise that in comprehending the other we have already 'invoked' him as other. In other words, comprehension depends on a relation prior to comprehension, a relation which does not involve knowing the other, but invokes him (Levinas, 6-7). The problem with this kind of relation is that it has no pragmatic value. If Morfydd listens to Porius she will invoke him as other, but she still won't know what he is talking about. With invocation alone, there can be no dialogue in the sense that 'dialogue' is usually understood.

Another problem with invocation is its reliance on language as the condition of our conscious grasp of the presence of the other. We have just seen that invocation of the other as other is of no pragmatic value, but if the invocation is in fact to be of the other as other, then the language by which the other is invoked must correspond to the other's being. This is contrary to pluralism. On the other hand, if the language by which the other is invoked is not referential, then we should not speak of invoking the other, but of producing what deconstruction calls the supplement.[4] While the other is that which is beyond my world version, the supplement exists within my world version, as a result of the fact that my world version is discursive and can be interpreted in different ways. Deconstruction can show that the supplementary interpretation of my discursive world version is as legitimate as the standard one, but this does not constitute dialogue (or any relation at all) with another world version. Other world versions exist beyond the site of the standard and supplementary interpretations, where there are other discourses, and there are things other than discourse (if we do not share Saussure's assumption). There is a big difference between belief in *différance* within discourse, which says that 'red chair' means both Mao and something you sit on, and belief in the otherness of other discourses, which says that 'red chair' is not equivalent to 'chaise rouge'. Otherness of discourses can only be overcome by dualism: translation relies on reference, in other words, on two discourses corresponding to the same reality.[5] Otherness than discourse is a dualist concept anyway.

Baudrillard recognises the difference between *différance*, which is 'otherness' – or more properly 'supplementarity' within discourse, and otherness, which is otherness of and otherness than discourse when he says that 'The radical Other is intolerable: he cannot be exterminated, but he cannot be accepted either, so the negotiable other, the other of difference, has to be promoted.' Young invites us to confuse *différance* with otherness when he says that Derrida 'articulates' the 'problematic' of the 'philosophical category of the centre' 'with the problem of Eurocentrism'.[6] Young's 'articulation with' is as ambiguous as his 'appropriation'. The same/ other oppositions of standard and supplementary interpretations and European and non-European nations, ethnicities and cultures can be spoken of together, but they cannot be compared. The idea in deconstruction that standard interpretations of texts illegitimately leave out supplementary interpretations cannot have anything to do with the material fact of colonialism, because if one did correspond to the other, then texts would be referential, and if texts were referential then the significance of texts could be limited to standard interpretations.

If we really did establish a relation with the other as other, we could regard such a relation as a deterritorialisation: an experience which cuts across the categories of body, mind and language. Deleuze and Guattari recognise the limitation of the deterritorial- isation offered by *différance* when they say that such a deterritorialisation occurs only on the plane of signification. This criticism is also extended to deterritorialisations which occur on the plane of subjectivity, and on the plane of the face. Either of these deterritorialisations could be seen as equivalent to Levinas's description of the invocation of the other, since Levinas's model of experience is centred on the subject, and since he says that the face-to-face relation establishes a relation with the other which avoids the 'ruse of the understanding' (in other words, a relation which invokes rather than comprehends). Yet while they criticise the limitations of these kinds of deterritorialisations, Deleuze and Guattari warn that they may be the only kinds available to us, given our present frame of reference.[7]

If our present frame of reference is a pluralist one, then Deleuze and Guattari are right. Levinas's model of a surplus of experience beyond any totality of knowledge is contrary to pluralism, since for pluralism there is no distinction between experience and knowledge: any deterritorialisation which occurs occurs in my world version (whether it is subjective or discursive) and is not prompted by anything outside my world version. Levinas, on the other hand, says that dialogue involves the calling into question of the same by the other. He assumes that the other is experienced beyond the totality of knowledge which comprises the same; in other words, that 'we exist in a circuit of understanding with reality'.[8] This circuit can be completed because there is experience before knowledge, or invocation before comprehension.

James also makes the dualist assumption of experience before knowledge when he describes the circuit of understanding. According to James, the pragmatist meaning of truth is that ideas are true insofar as they help us get into satisfactory relation with other parts of our experience. The pluralist response to this is, 'what other parts'? Similarly, pragmatism says that a person changes his opinions in response to 'an inward trouble to which his mind till then had been a stranger', a trouble caused by new experience. The pluralist response is 'there is no experience beyond opinions'. James may well be talking about a distinction between theory and personal knowledge here, but as we saw earlier, this is not a useful distinction for pluralism.[9]

The other is a problem for pluralism, because two key assumptions of pluralism are firstly that there are many world versions, and secondly that I only have access to one world version. If we accept these assumptions then we accept that there is an other, but also that we can never know, comprehend or invoke the other. Within the wall which surrounds our world version, we tell ourselves a story which says that there are other world versions beyond the wall, but we can never look over the wall to check if this story is true. So while Hooker is right to say that Powys has 'a weak sense of the "other"',[10] a 'weak sense' of the other is all that a pluralist can claim to have. Our relation to the other is 'weak' in Vattimo's sense, because for us the other is fictional rather than factual, our story of world versions beyond the wall remains a story.[11]

It is this 'weak sense' of the other which Powys describes when Porius is holding up Myrddin. What Porius holds is the experience of plurality, the experience which shows him that

> it was possible to enlarge a person's identity till it embraced other identities, till it could escape at will *into others,* till it could even discover that all the while beneath the obstinate opacity of itself, it was on the verge of becoming these others (66).

This is an experience in line with the first assumption of pluralism, the assumption that there are many world versions. But the second assumption, that I can only know one world version, is not forgotten. Porius does not have dialogue, he thinks about dialogue. In Powys's words, he 'dimly tracks down' a 'devious thought' which 'has to do' with the 'possibility' that the self can be 'on the verge' of becoming other. When Bhabha says that 'We need to be aware... that we remain conscious of the ethical choice of our existence: to represent the 'other's' difference within my own [*sic*]',[12] he, like Powys, uses images of thoughts contained within thoughts to create a sense of separation between the other in fact and the other in our fictional weak sense of it, though in Bhabha's case this separation may be inadvert.

Porius decides he must never forget the experience he has got hold of by getting hold of Myrddin, then wonders, 'But what had he got? Anyway, it was the extreme opposite of what Minnawc Gorsant preached every night' (66). Having acknowledged he does not know Myrddin as Myrddin, he appropriates him as part of a totalising philosophical opposition between pluralism and dualism. Of course, Myrddin does represent pluralism, and Minnawc does represent dualism, but by saying 'it was' Porius is ignoring the surplus which constitutes Myrddin's otherness. He is collapsing what Myrddin is into what Myrddin represents for him. According to pluralism, this is all he can do, since pluralism collapses being and knowledge. Only in the question, 'what had he got?' is there a sense that Myrddin could be other than how Porius knows him, ad 'what had he got?' is an acknowledgement of a lack of knowledge. For pluralism, the other is what we do not know, and Medrawd acknowledges Porius's otherness when Porius asks him '"What am I?"' and he replies '"I don't know"' (599).

On several other occasions in *Porius*, dialogue is promised and then problematised in a similar way. Porius thinks of the self and the body as terms in an 'I-you' relation (841). The expression 'I-you' promises dialogue along the lines of Buber's 'I-thou' relation, which, like Levinas's invocation, is a relation to the other as other. Buber says that 'When *Thou* is spoken, the speaker has no thing

for his object', 'he takes his stand in relation'.[13] Porius's
'cavoseniargizing' is an experience in which this relation seems to
be realised, in which he 'bridges' the gulf between 'the animal
consciousness of his body... and the consciousness of his... soul',
'so that his soul found itself able to follow every curve and ripple
of his bodily sensations *and yet remain suspended above them*', like
oil flowing above water (87).

The problem with this description is that 'so that' argues for a
causality which is contrary to the implications of the figures. The
figure of the bridge and the figure of oil above water have very
different connotations. If the soul-body opposition was bridged
then soul and body would flow into one another, not one above
the other. Bridging implies dialogue, and oil above water does
not. The difference in the figures points to two different ways of
interpreting cavoseniargizing. How does Porius know that his
soul follows his body; in other words, that his thought follows his
sensations, unless he knows what those sensations are independently of thought? If he does know this, then the relation between
them is one of correspondence: it is dualist, and the bridge is an
accurate figure. If he does not know this, then there is no way for
him to know whether his thought follows his sensations, since all
he knows of the sensations is produced by thought. This is
pluralism, and oil above water is an accurate figure.

Taliesin also seems to establish a self-other relation, while he is
staring at a straw. Powys tells us that gradually 'a relation began
to establish itself between the man in his quiescence on the warm
dry stool and the straw in its quiescence on the damp ground'.
This relation is such that Taliesin 'seemed to share' his immediate
experiences 'on something like equal terms with his unresponsive
fellow-tellurian'. He is said to say '"you and I"' to the straw (429).
Despite the terms, which again are similar to Buber's, the relation
is problematised by Powys's use of 'seemed' and 'unresponsive'.
Taliesin might seem to share experiences with the straw, but as

the straw does not respond to him, no dialogue actually takes place except at the level of seeming; in other words, the sharing takes place within a particular world version (presumably Taliesin's), not between world versions: this kind of sharing is not dialogue.

Though Powys often describes experience in very particular ways in *Porius* the experience usually turns out to be someone's particular experience, rather than the experience of something particular: in other words, it takes place within a particular world version. For example, when Powys gives a long description of Porius's experience of the colour of corn stubble in the afternoon light, he stresses the strangeness of the colour, and the difficulty Porius has naming it (5-7). This seems to be a good example of Levinas's surplus, of the other as an experience which exceeds our ability to know it. Later, though, Porius realises that the reason why he is so impressed with this particular colour is that it is the colour which a patch of Morfydd's forehead sometimes turns (13). In fact

> He had come to associate the poignancy of her abandonment to pity and wrath so completely with this particular token that the sight of this stubble-field burdening the mist called up in him all those old familiar feelings with which, since the days when she was five and Rhun was fifteen and he was ten, he was wont to quiet her emotion (14).

What seemed to be other is seen to be the same. The only reason Porius experiences the colour at all is because it is already an important part of his world version. It is important, not in itself, but for him.

There is no dialogue in *Porius*, though the impulse towards dialogue, as Porius's cavoseniargizing shows, is strong. There is, though, plenty of dialogism, in other words, Powys often makes juxtapositions of incommensurable world versions. For Powys, there are as many 'other' world versions as there are other entities: in *All or Nothing* the Cerne Giant says that even empty space has 'a self of its own, a self that says, "I am I," and to whom everything else in the entire universe is either a "you" or an "it"' (AN, 190). In *Porius*, world versions are given not only to all the human characters, but also to a dog, midges and beetles, and of course Taliesin's straw (23, 133, 429). The effect of this multiplicity of versions is to undermine the idea that any is to be privileged over any of the others. On page 195, for example, Euronwy explains her motives to Morfydd, which allows the reader to see events from her point of view. At the same time, the scene is focalised via Morfydd, so we see events from her point of view as well.

By multiplying points of view, Powys follows the first assumption of pluralism, which is that there are many world versions. He also follows the second assumption, which is that each person can only know one world version. Though Morfydd's focalisation includes Euronwy's explanation of her motives, Morfydd has no dialogue with Euronwy: she cannot understand her. This is shown by the fact that Morfydd suggests that she and Euronwy make their promise to each other 'on' that which they each hold most sacred: for her, this is the ruins of Rhitta Gawr and for Euronwy it is the altar of Christ (197). This is a pluralist way of pledging allegiance in which two subjects can commit themselves to each other without having a dialogue: they are only committed from their own point of view. The true test of the other's commitment to you is not whether he will do something which *you* think is a sacrifice, but whether he will do something which *he* thinks is a sacrifice.

This focus on subjective world versions is what makes *Porius* a novel of experiences rather than of actions. As Cadawg waits for Tonwen to get into his boat, he experiences

one of the decisive moments of his long life. What practical decision he himself now made, as a result of this climax to more than a century of personal impressions, he would have been hard put to say, but the experience itself, though a concaten-ation of several minute particulars, was a clear and definite one (338).

It is this kind of experience, which may not have any practical consequences, but which is nonetheless important to the person who has it, which Powys chooses to focus on throughout the novel. This approach is consistent with subjective pluralism, since where action is important from the point of view of the community, experience is important from the point of view of the individual.

As Morfydd and Euronwy's promises indicate, actions which do involve two or more individuals are understood differently from each individual's point of view. Powys is more explicit about this when he describes Rhun attempting to rape Morfydd. As Morfydd wakes up, Powys tells us that 'a new and opposed world had rushed into this particular oasis of time and space, where it confronted the one that was already in possession' (468). Powys emphasises the conflict between the two characters' world versions, telling us that 'His anger was as burning as hers was cold' (470). This conflict is also expressed in the change of style halfway through the description of Rhun jumping on top of Morfydd. Powys says

> What is certain is that the raptorial beauty of the almost feline leap which the unequalled muscles of this son of a Greek athlete made possible, as Rhun exchanged the cold floor of the upper chamber of Ty Cerrig for the bed of his foster-brother's bride, passed unseen and unrecognised by its would-be prey. Of one feeling alone was Morfydd conscious, as with all her strength she flung him off, flung him back, flung him away, flung him down with such unexpected violence, that, entangled in the purple blanket and thus unable to retain his balance, he fell with a thud that made a sound upon the stone floor not unpleasant to her ice-cold anger (470).

Here the periphrasis in the description of Rhun's jump creates an expectation of heroism which grows through several clauses, and is then abruptly deflated at the end of the first sentence. The style then changes, the straightforward diction and repeats of 'flung him' are expressive of Morfydd's single-mindedness. Rhun is equally single-minded, but his 'red-black world that contained nothing but the image of a smoking spear of phallic fury rushing upon a resistant blur of whiteness' (471) is completely different from Morfydd's world version. Powys continues to make this conflict an explicit comment on the plurality of world versions, firstly by introducing Lot-el-Azziz as a hypothetical observer of the action. Had he been there, says Powys, Lot 'would have quoted his favourite Rabbi to the effect that every living creature – from insects so small as to be invisible to human eyesight, to huge pythons and sea-serpents – holds in its consciousness a whole universe, perhaps more than a universe' (471). Secondly, Powys's description of the interruption of Rhun's assault by Gwrgi and Canna uses the terms of the world version theme: Powys tells us that Rhun's lustful world version is 'brought to an end by the concatenation of two other worlds of human consciousness' (471).

The heroic description of Rhun's leap which turns out to be redundant because it is incommensurable with Morfydd's world version, and the theory that every consciousness holds a universe which can be introduced only via an observer who is brought onto the scene courtesy of a type three conditional (something which could have happened but did not), are examples of two common Powys devices, the anticlimax, and the hypothetical observer. The effect of both devices is to indicate that as far as Powys is concerned, everything *is* only inasmuch as it is *known* by someone. This goes for Powys's novel too. The fictional world of *Porius* is, inasmuch as we know it, inasmuch as Powys tells us about it. According to the first assumption of pluralism, there are many other versions of *Porius*, but according to the second assumption of pluralism, Powys can only tell us about a single version. In order to remain consistently pluralist, he needs to

54

create a weak sense of other versions of *Porius* without telling us about them. If he did tell us about them, they would become part of his world version. When stories (such as those in Robert Coover's *Pricksongs and Descants*) contain several incommensurable versions of the same plot, these plot versions cannot be said to be in dialogue with each other, since they are all part of the same story, which is itself a single world version. As Young says, 'The structure of dialogue... disallows the taking up of any position beyond the interlocutors from which they can be integrated into a larger totality'.[14]

Powys creates a weak sense of other versions of *Porius* by using what Bakhtin calls a 'double-voiced' style. Double-voiced narration is directed both towards its object (in this case, the fictional world of Porius) and towards someone else's speech (in this case, what someone else might tell us about the fictional world of *Porius*).[15] As I showed in "What is the Saturnian Quest?" we are continually made aware of Powys as a subject producing a version of *Porius*. This means that we are also aware that other subjects could produce other versions of *Porius*. We are given a weak sense of these other versions, though we never know them.

This account of reading *Porius* assumes that we know about the fictional world of *Porius* inasmuch as Powys tells us about it, but this assumption is not consistent with pluralism. I have said that Powys's version of *Porius* creates a weak sense of other versions of that fictional world, but to be consistent with pluralism I should say that *my* version of Powys's version creates a weak sense of other versions, since other versions of Powys's version may not agree that Powys's performative style makes us aware that he is a subject producing a version, and/ or may not agree that our awareness that he is a subject producing a version leads to a further awareness that other subjects could produce other versions.

According to pluralism, the characters, the writer and the reader of *Porius* have no way of experiencing other world versions beyond the wall which surrounds their own world version, and no way of experiencing other versions of *Porius*. Myrddin says it would be wiser not to understand him, but it would be wisest, from a pluralist perspective, to *recognise* that we cannot understand Myrddin, since the moment we understand his world version it ceases to be his world version and becomes ours. For Levinas, we must avoid the ruse of understanding, because understanding the other makes the other part of the same, so once the other is understood, it is no longer other. It would be wise of Morfydd to recognise that she cannot understand Porius's world version without it ceasing to be his world version, and wise of us to recognise that in understanding *Porius*, we are not understanding Powys's *Porius*.

Three

Performativity in *Owen Glendower*

In the first essay I described pluralism as the belief that being and knowledge are not separate categories. In postmodernist theory, an important subcategory of the collapse of the distinction between being and knowing is the collapse of the distinction between what is real and what is performed. The most explicit and influential account of the collapse of this distinction has been Judith Butler's *Gender Trouble*. In this book, Butler asserts that 'There is no gender identity behind the expressions of gender; that identity is performatively constituted by the very "expressions" that are said to be its results.'[1]

Butler's use of the word 'performative' here points to a link between postmodernist theories of performance and J. L. Austin's theory of performative speech acts. Austin distinguishes between constative utterances, which are utterances about something, are implicitly testable by correspondence to that something, and thus imply an opposition of knowing and being, and performative utterances, which are not utterances about something, but are rather utterances which enact something.[2] In the context of Austin's distinction, Butler's contention is that expressions of gender cannot be constative, they can only be performative. Jonathan Culler goes further when he suggests that all constatives can be seen as performatives whose explicit performative verb has been deleted.[3]

The collapse of the constative into the performative, and the consequent rejection of the idea that any utterance is about something and therefore testable by correspondence to that something, does not occur in *How To Do Things With Words*. In fact, Austin says there that he agrees that the question of the truth or falsity of an utterance is 'the question of whether the statement "corresponds with the facts". What Austin does say is that his own categories of constative and performative are abstractions which are not very expedient, and that one of the reasons for this is that 'When a constative is confronted with the facts, we in fact appraise it in ways involving the employment of a vast array of terms which overlap with those that we use in the appraisal of performatives.' In other words, both constatives and performatives can be appraised in terms of their correspondence to facts. In real life, as Austin says, the appraisal is usually not a simple test of truth or falsity, but it is a correspondence test nevertheless. This can be seen in the case of Austin's own examples, the utterances 'France is hexagonal', 'Lord Raglan won the battle of Alma', and 'all snow geese migrate to Labrador'. These utterances are not simply true or false, they are rather 'suitable to some contexts and not to others'.[4] Still, what makes them suitable to some contexts and not to others is their level of correspondence to the facts. If I were to say that Bronson Pinchot won the battle of Alma, this would be unsuitable to contexts where 'Lord Raglan won the battle of Alma' is suitable, and the difference is down to a difference in correspondence with the facts.

Austin's point is that for both constatives and performatives, whether or not an utterance is right and proper is dependent in part 'on the facts'. This is the case with the performative utterance to the effect that the batsman is out.[5] The utterance is performative in the sense that the batsman is out because the umpire says he is, but it is also testable by correspondence to the facts. If an umpire gives a batsman out when the batsman *was not out*, his utterance will not have been right and proper. Of course, in terms of the game of cricket, it is the umpire's decision which finally counts, not whether or not the batsman *was* or *was not* out, but if this element of correspondence testing were not involved in appraising umpires' decisions, there would be no dissent, no recourse to TV replays and to the third umpire, no neutral umpires, etc.

On this reading, Austin's attitude to performativity is very different from Butler and Culler's attitudes, and to the postmodernist attitude I have taken their attitudes to represent. Austin retains the notion of correspondence, and it is the fact that both constatives and performatives can be tested for correspondence which leads him to question his own distinction between the two. Postmodernist theory retains Austin's initial distinction between constatives and performatives, then argues that all utterances are really performatives, and consequently questions the notion of correspondence. For postmodernist theory, the fact that all utterances are really performatives means that we must accept that the batsman is out because the umpire says he is, rather than assuming that the umpire said the batsman was out because he thought he was, and looking to the facts to test the umpire's utterance. Baudrillard implies that in the postmodern society all utterances are performative when he says that

All our categories have thus entered the age of the factitious: no more wanting – only getting people to want; no more doing – only getting people to do; no more *being worth* something – merely getting something to be worth something (witness advertising in general); no more knowing – only letting know.[6]

The performative (as it is when Austin initially defines it, rather than as it is on his subsequent examination of it) is not testable by correspondence, and similarly for Baudrillard in postmodern society 'there are no lies, *there is only simulation,* which is precisely the facticity of facts'.[7] While facticity (in other words, performativity) is an aspect of postmodern society which Baudrillard is diagnosing, Richard Palmer advocates performativity as a postmodernist strategy, saying that 'emphasis on verifiable truth and correctness can lead to an insensitivity to the performative *doing* that takes place in *saying*'.[8]

Where postmodernist theory regards utterances as performative and collapses the distinction between real events and performances, it is at odds with traditional history, and traditional historical fiction, which are concerned to separate reality from performance. One example of this separation occurs in a historical novel of failed nationalist rebellion in many respects similar to Powys's *Owen Glendower,* Walter Scott's *Redgauntlet.* Scott sets up an initial opposition between performance and reality in his introduction, referring to Charles Stuart's rebellion as 'circumstances fascinating to the imagination, [which] might well be supposed to seduce young and enthusiastic minds to the cause in which they were found united, although wisdom and reason frowned upon the enterprise.'[9] The implication that Darsie is liable to be seduced by the enterprise of his Jacobite uncle Redgauntlet is continued in the novel itself by Alan Fairford, who warns him, 'See not a Dulcinea in every slipshod girl', tells him not to let his imagination run away with him, and makes his own role more explicit by saying '"I will be your faithful Sancho Panza"' (Scott, 23, 58, 123). Despite these allusions, however, there is little chance that Darsie will be seduced by the Jacobite fiction in the same way as Quixote is seduced by the chivalric fiction. He says himself, 'I could have been well contented to have swopped the romance of my situation, together with the glorious independence of control which I possessed at the moment, for the comforts of the chimney-corner' (Scott, 39-40).

Though it threatens to upset the accepted political realities of post-'45 Scotland with the romance of a new Jacobite rebellion, *Redgauntlet* contains its own threat by using allusions to *Don Quixote* to indicate that the rebellion is a romance, and that if Darsie were to believe in it, his belief would have no more substance than Quixote's belief in the chivalric fiction. In other words, Scott's novel contains the Jacobite threat by treating it as a performative. The English forces in Scott's novel do something very similar. The King commands that Greenmantle's gesture of laying down the gauntlet at his coronation 'should not be farther enquired into' (Scott, 519), and after the new Jacobite rebellion has failed, Campbell pardons all the new rebels and pretends that nothing has happened (Scott, 627). In both cases, the Jacobite gesture is treated as if it did not correspond to a real threat, and as if the threat exists only by virtue of the gesture. By ignoring the gesture, the English destroy the threat. Again, Scott's novel accepts that this is the case, and consequently that the gestures of rebellion are performative: when he is told that everyone has been pardoned, even Redgauntlet recognises that '"the cause is lost forever!"' (Scott, 628)

A postmodernist reading of *Redgauntlet* could be expected to demonstrate how the accepted political reality of the novel is as performative as the threatened Jacobite rebellion, and how the process of containment I have described is not a reality to which Scott's utterances correspond, but is itself constructed by those utterances. The postmodernist historical novel is similarly concerned to problematise all accounts of how things were, such that all accounts have equal status as performatives. Jameson says that 'This historical novel [he is talking specifically about E. L.

Doctorow's *Ragtime*] can no longer set out to represent the historical past; it can only "represent" our ideas and stereotypes about that past' (Jameson, 25). In his epigraph to *In the Skin of a Lion*, Michael Ondaatje, quoting John Berger, tells us 'Never again will a single story be told as though it were the only one.'[10]

Ian Duncan sees *Owen Glendower* as a traditional historical novel, in which the real and the performative are separated. He sees this separation as occurring first in 'the defeat of the imagination' which occurs when Rhisiart sees the difference between the Dinas Bran of his imagination and the real Dinas Bran.[11] In fact, though Rhisiart is afraid of precisely this kind of disillusionment, worrying that the real Dinas Bran will make his imagined one 'dissolve into air' (9), when he first sees the castle it is *'more'*, not 'less', than the picture he has in his mind (12). In particular, it is more marvellous, less realistic, than he has imagined it: it has the look of 'some far-away fairy tower in some old pre-druidic Book of Revelation' (12).

As this example suggests, my interpretation of *Owen Glendower* is opposed to Duncan's. I think that Powys's novel works in a way which is quite different from *Redgauntlet*, and which is analogous to postmodernist theory and postmodernist novels. I think that in *Owen Glendower*, we are continually reminded that identities, and events, are performative, that is, they are constituted by the expressions which might otherwise be taken to correspond to them. I also think that Powys's techniques continually remind us that the world in which these identities and events exist, though labelled 'historical', is itself performative, constituted by Powys's words.

Though R.R. Davies looks to separate myth from real events in his own history of Owain's rebellion (for example, in his account of Dafydd Gam) he also says that it is unwise to discount the power of myth as an influence on the real events he is writing about.[12] He picks out specific aspects of the rebellion which illustrate the importance of performance in determining policy, arguing, for example, that it is on the basis of Welsh political mythology rather than Welsh political reality that Owain is able to 'cast himself as the deliverer' of Wales, and as the 'rightful heir' of Owain Lawgoch (Davies, 90, 160-1). In Powys's novel, this performative aspect of Owen's rebellion is emphasised. When he proclaims himself Prince of Wales, Owen thinks to himself '"What I'm doing now [...] won't only mean ashes and blood. It'll mean mumming and miming and play-acting and masquerading, till a man's heart run's sick!"' (399).[13] Accordingly, after Rhisiart has insulted Gilles de Pirogue, Owen determines to '"unloose this knot by a little stage play"' (652), which he later sees as 'absurd play-acting' (668).

Though these references indicate that Owen sees the performative aspect of his rebellion as a distasteful but unavoidable necessity (something which, like Scott's romance of a Jacobite rebellion, can be separated from and unfavourably compared to the reality of rebellion as represented by 'ashes and blood'), elsewhere Owen's use of performance is seen to take precedence over what appears to be the practical course of action. Griffith Young, for example, calls Owen a '"play-acting fool!"' (148), refers to his '"mummeries"' (149), and says that Owen has lost his chance 'by telling the world what he's going to do' (169). Young is right: Owen is committed to performance at the expense of what is practical. He will not, for example, start the uprising until September 16th because Iolo Goch said that that was the right date (203).

The most significant example of this commitment to performance at the expense of the practical occurs after Hopkin has predicted the anointing of a king by a 'victorious "virgin in armour"' (637-8), Owen decides that 'That's what he wanted, that's what Wales wanted at this juncture, some moving bardic symbol, at once poetic and religious!"' (638). He imagines a future in which he rides to London to be crowned king, with Tegolin in golden armour by his side (648). It is the allure of this image which prevents him stopping the war by doing homage to the English king (651).

Owen's commitment to performance is shown not to be a case of doing what needs to be done, but a case of doing what he wants to do. Performance is part of his character. His behaviour is distinguished by its 'ritualistic courtliness' (179) and 'effusive ceremony' (180). He has been brought up in an 'elaborate and fantastical code of courtesy' (404). Our first view of Owen is focused on his appearance, his clothing and his beard (120). He is said to take a 'great deal of pains to enhance his princely appearance' (391), but the result of these pains is that he looks marvellous, not realistic: Powys tells us that his turned-up boots are 'fantastical' and 'ridiculous' (390-1), and later that he is wearing 'almost fantastically gorgeous attire' (511).

It is not just Owen who is performative. In *Owen Glendower*, performativity is part of the Welsh national character. At Glyndyfrdwy, even events which are spontaneous appear as performances: Powys tells us that, 'Every man in the hall, following Owen with the rhythmic consentaneousness of a familiar ritual, repeated the words he had used; and, after that, with a moment as spontaneous as if it had been practised for a thousand years, they lifted their cups to their lips' (146-7). At Dinas Bran too, there is an example of spontaneity appearing as performance: Denis Burnell orders that pipe-notes be played, then all the Welshmen in the hall say an 'archaic Welsh rhyme', after which the women proceed two by two towards the door (348-9).

It is not just the Welsh who are performative in *Owen Glendower*. Owen's son Griffith '"hates his Welsh blood"' (167), but in order to mock Welsh nationalism, he wears the belt of King Eliseg around his neck: even his dissent from the performativity of the rebellion is itself performed. Though the 'extravagant airs' of the

Pope's emissary are amusing to the 'English' Rhisiart, Brut and Young (191), each of these three characters is seen to engage in performance. When Rhisiart is hostaged to Valle Crucis he 'thinks out' the 'exact line' he's going to take, which is to make a lot of being one of the family and of being a law student from Oxford (212). Later he adopts a guileless expression to encourage Adda to tell him more about the political situation than he would do otherwise (317). When Walter Brut warns Rhisiart of the dangers of flirtations with pages, 'deliberately' uses 'the rustic Herefordshire dialect, giving a touch of nostalgic homeliness to his elder brother's tone' (198). Though Young criticises Owen's attachment to performance, he himself thinks in terms of performance, telling Rhisiart that Owen would '"be fitter for the part... if he would listen more and think less"' (143).

Young's inconsistency illustrates the ubiquity of performance in *Owen Glendower*. He does not think that Owen should stop playing a role, rather, he thinks that Owen should stop playing a role which is obviously a performance. In fact, it is not an option in *Owen Glendower* for characters to stop playing roles and just 'be themselves'. This ubiquity of performance is established in Powys's first descriptions of Rhisiart, which present him as a collection of signs which do not correspond to an underlying reality. His sword is out of date, more for show that for use (3), and its sheath is embossed and enamelled (13). His horse's straps are 'gilded' (3) and the horse itself looks so 'peculiar' that Welshpool prentices raise the cry of '"mummers"' when they see Rhisiart at Hereford (4). Later we find out that the horse is an 'old pageant-horse' (418).

Rhisiart's activity on this first appearance is principally imaginative, that is, principally concerned with the construction of more signs which do not correspond to reality. He imagines a meeting with Owen, at which he has with him 'his piebald horse, his crusader's sword, and his coat of chain-armour' (10). Not only is the meeting performative, but it involves the other performatives by which Rhisiart has been defined. He imagines Dinas Bran, and when he sees it, and it is even less realistic than he has imagined it, he goes through a 'ritualistic performance' (13). He imagines rescuing Tegolin before he knows who she is or what is happening to her (23-24). As he rides to her rescue, he tells himself 'one fantastic story after another' (28). When he draws his sword and rides forward towards Mad Huw through the bowmen, he does so because he has been used to doing it in play: pretending he is rescuing Dinas Bran (44-45) is one of his many 'little private rituals' (206). When he finally sees Owen, 'the Owen he saw that day took his place, naturally and with a fatal inevitableness, on the ramparts of Dinas Bran and gathered into himself their mystic enchantment' (122). In other words, as with Dinas Bran, when Rhisiart is confronted with the real counterpart of an object of his imagination, the imagined object is not replaced by the real object, instead, the real object is included in the imagined object. This is just the kind of inclusion in which the constative turns out to be performative that we saw in postmodernist theory.

There are several other occasions in *Owen Glendower* when constatives turn out to be performatives. The dying nurse, for example, objects to seeing any priest but Mad Huw, and calls Father Pascentius a 'monking monk from a monkery of mummers' (576). Nevertheless, by a piece of play-acting, Father Rheinalt is able to give her the last rites: he has just been fishing, arrives with his fishing gear, and pretends he is St. Peter. It is Broch O' Meifod's idea, but Broch says, '"The lie wasn't mine [...] *the lie was life's*"' (580). Constative also turns out to be performative when Owen cuts himself in the throat. Broch tells Rhisiart, '"he's *not* dead. Nor is he in the least danger of dying. He's only been play-acting for conscience-sake"' (610). Nevertheless, this performance is, according to Powys, 'real enough' to work its purpose in making Owen feel remorse (619), just as Father Rheinalt's performance as St. Peter is real enough to give the nurse the last rites, and to be said by Broch to be part of life.

Broch is most explicit about the collapse of reality into performativity when he tells Owen '"We may be play-actors before each other, night and day, for fifty year; but a time comes when we have to act our part *for ourselves alone*"' (785). This statement is a powerful example of the attitude that everything is performative, because we expect the second clause of Broch's sentence to say the opposite of what it does say. We expect it to move from the admission of performance to the acceptance of reality, but in fact it simply moves from performance to performance. Just as when Rhisiart sees the real Dinas Bran, and the real Owen, where we expected to find the truth, we find another illusion. This is also the case with Iago. Iago is the representative of realism in the novel, telling Elphin, '"This is real war. We're seeing a real battle!"' (814), but even his 'downright soldier-look, so blunt and unaffected', is said to be something he 'assumes', because he is carrying a spear (807).

The implication of the constant grounding in performance, even at points in the novel where we would expect assertions of the real, is that there is no real, there is nothing except performance. This is a central idea in postmodernist theory. Campbell Tatham says, for example, 'if I sit down before my mirrors in order to remove my make-up only to discover yet another layer of emptiness at the presumed core [...] I need not despair: we can always create a new role, initiate a new performance',[14] but it is also a central idea in *Owen Glendower*. The parallel between Powys and Tatham is clear when Powys describes

> the dangerous clear air of the hour before dawn, when the nature-nourished *illusions*, upon which the life of all living things depend [*sic*], grow thin and transparent, leaving nearly bare that naked reality

which the Great Mother so tenderly pats and plasters with her imperishable pretences (677).

Tatham describes a combination of emptiness under performances, and a consequent ability to change the roles which are performed, and it is just this combination which we find in Powys's characters, and particularly in *Owen Glendower*. There is a glimpse of this emptiness in Owen and Meredith when we see 'a look pass between them of such weary amusement that everything else in that smoky hall faded away, and the man with the forked beard and the man with the black curls created between them a gulf of intellectual detachment into which all the fever of life sank' (146). Powys later tells us that there is a deep 'abnormality' behind Owen's 'courtly façade', a detachment from all normal emotions (361). It is this detachment which allows him to abandon himself to the role of Prince of Wales, to what he sees as an 'inescapable obedience to the event' (562).

We see this obedience to the event, this abandonment to the role, on the day Owen proclaims himself Prince of Wales. Powys tells us that Owen does not know '"*to what end*"' he is rebelling (395). This sense that the rebellion as performance does not correspond to anything real, either any real fact of Owen's rightful Princeship or any real political aim, is emphasised by the ramshackle nature of the performance itself. Owen's standard is wrong (it has a gold dragon, not a red one) and his throne is 'ricketty [*sic*]' (396). Later, when Owen has set up a court, that court is equally performative: the court is 'motley' (448), its courtiers are makeshift: Rhisiart is transformed into a 'Secretary', Brut into a 'Librarian', and even Simon the Hog 'played the armourer' (466). Owen's own role as 'Prince' is something he can put on and take off: walking away from the crowd watching the comet, he 'instantly dropped the prince and became in a second a hunted outlaw, a native of caves and forests!' (475).

This ability to change roles, which again points to the fact that none of the roles corresponds to an underlying real identity, is seen as Owen's particular skill. When he is preparing to go into battle accompanied by the maid in armour, he draws attention away from himself (and consequently draws attention to Tegolin) by riding an insignificant horse and wearing all black (694). Earlier on he is seen to disguise himself, attending the meeting at Dinas Bran wearing a false beard and disguised as a lay brother (378). Yet Owen is not the only character who is said to change his identity: early on, riding to the aid of Tegolin and Mad Huw, John ap Hywel changes so that Rhisiart sees, 'in place of a mystical ascetic [...] an excited warrior' (28). As Rhisiart himself arrives at Glyndyfrdwy, Powys says that 'with each step he took there seemed to fall away from him a great segment of his past identity' (124). In Catherine's own mind, her identity becomes conflated with the wood-nymph of her imaginary world (504). It seems that no character has a fixed, stable, real identity beneath the roles they play.

If we accept the position implied in *Owen Glendower*, that constatives turn out to be performatives, this helps us make sense of one of the most puzzling aspects of the novel, which is Owen's decision not to storm the city of Worcester. Though the decision makes no practical sense – even after the retreat from Worcester, Rhisiart is confidently telling Walter Brut that '"One thing is certain... Owen'll never retreat, now he has once made the plunge!"' (827), it can be shown to make sense in a world where the performative is prioritised, a world in which Owen's identity as Prince of Wales is a role and his rebellion is a performance.

The two histories Powys probably used as sources for his novel both present the retreat from Worcester as a practical decision. In Wylie, Owen and Henry arrive at Worcester at the same time, taking up strong positions on opposite sides of a valley. It is implicit that because both sides are in strong positions, neither side is willing to attack. Finally, it is 'want of provisions and forage' which causes the Welsh and French forces to retreat. In Lloyd, Owen's forces arrive at Worcester first, and wait for Henry to arrive. After Henry arrives, there is a week of stand-off, after which Owen retreats because he has 'overshot the mark, venturing too far into a hostile country', in which he cannot 'renew his supplies.'[15]

In Powys's novel, Henry arrives at Worcester before Owen, there is a stand-off, and then Owen retreats (820-3). Unlike Wylie and Lloyd, Powys raises the question of why Owen did not attack Worcester straight away. Owen asks himself 'Why *hadn't* h e stormed the city at once?' (820). Powys shows that the answer lies in Owen's unusual quality of being able to shift his position so that any situation seems like a performance. In this case, his shift of position leads him to see his own invasion as a performance.

Before arriving at Woodbury Hill, Owen has already begun to feel that he has made a mistake. This feeling centres on the idea that he should have secured the independence of Wales by bargaining with Henry, rather than expanding the rebellion beyond Wales to include the French, the Mortimers and the Percies (811-2). His uncertainty intensifies shortly before the Welsh and the French reach Woodbury Hill, when the French soldiers go on a spree of looting, raping and burning in an English village. Though this scene leads Iago to tell Elphin that '"This is real war"' (814), it also leads Owen to view his invasion as a performance. He thinks

> "Something's come over me, [...] but what it is – Dewi Sant! *I* don't know! I feel as if Bolingbroke and I were tilting at each other in one of Richard's fancy tourneys. I feel as if even the crown in London wasn't worth –" (819).

After he has watched the ravaging of the village, Owen feels that there is 'something more *real* about the way it was cropping the grass out there than about all this marching and countermarching; yes! more real, and with more life in it!' (820). Powys says that it is this feeling which causes Owen not to storm Worcester, that

> The savagery he'd seen in the burning of that unlucky village had bruised something in the depths of his nature; and it was this bruise, though he dodged it and avoided facing it, that had covered up *that* road [the road to London, via Worcester] (820-1).

The realities of fighting come to seem like a performance to Owen, and the practicalities of rebellion are consequently reduced to 'fantastic tales' which he tells himself about taking both Henrys prisoner and demanding the crown of England as their ransom (821). What instead comes to be seen as the valuable aspect of the rebellion is its performative aspect. The rebellion of the Welsh in *Owen Glendower* is no more practically effective than the rebellion of the Jacobites in *Redgauntlet*. But in terms of the rhetorical structure of the two novels – because Powys emphasises the importance of the performative throughout his novel, whereas Scott de-emphasises the importance of the performative throughout his – the Welsh rebellion is privileged where the Jacobite is not. This difference is seen in the response of the rebels to the practical failure of their efforts. Whereas Redgauntlet says '"the cause is lost forever"' (Scott, 628), Owen tells his grandson Rhisiart that

> "The story of Glyn Dwr will be a story for all the Welshmen who come afterwards – to the end of time! And in no other land in the wide world save Wales could it have happened. That's what we Welshmen are! They may conquer us in arms, they may out-wit us in trade, they may out-mode us in fashions of science and art. One thing they cannot do. They cannot *catch our souls*!" (886).

Like Owen, Powys attributes to the Welsh national character a special quality, the quality of not being caught, or rather, not being pinned down to a particular position. For Powys, where 'Other races love and hate, conquer and are conquered', 'This race avoids and evades, pursues and is pursued' (889), 'You cannot force it to love you or to hate you. You can only watch it escaping from you' (890). The special quality of the Welsh national character could therefore be said to be performativity. Signs of Welsh identity are not constative, they do not correspond to a fixed, immutable reality which participates in struggles for power, they are performative, they turn out to construct the identity of which they would otherwise be presumed to be the expression. The Welsh identity, like Owen's identity, cannot be pinned down because it is whatever it appears to be.

In not storming Worcester, in being able to revision the practicalities of rebellion as performative, Owen exemplifies the Welsh character as Powys defines it here. Having pursued his rebellion of '"ashes and blood"' as far as Worcester, Owen is able suddenly to look at that rebellion again, and see it as a thing of '"mumming and miming and play-acting and masquerading"', and give it up. Because he is able to do this, because his roles have an emptiness behind them, we cannot catch his soul. His rebellion, and in particular his decision not to storm Worcester, exemplifies the Welsh national character as he has defined it, and as Powys has defined it, because its constatives turn out to be performatives. His rebellion – and again in particular his decision not to storm Worcester – and the Welsh national character which his rebellion exemplifies, are in turn privileged within the rhetorical structure of Powys's novel, which itself implies that constatives turn out to be performatives.

Powys supports this conclusion that in terms of the rhetorical structure of the novel, and in terms of the Welsh national identity, the retreat from Worcester is the right and proper conclusion to the rebellion, by preparing for the retreat during the novel. When he is describing Mathrafal to Rhisiart and Efa, Owen undergoes a form of collapse, during which he feels that he is looking 'into another dimension of life' (415). Yet immediately afterwards he thinks to himself, '"everything I did just now, even to hugging my horse's neck, even to letting myself collapse, was deliberate"' (416). On several other important occasions in the novel, Owen breaks off what he is saying or doing and undergoes a similar form of collapse: for example, it is during one of his collapses that the French begin ravaging the village outside Worcester (813-4). These collapses involve a loss of practical power, a shift of frame of reference by which the immediate reality is made to seem unreal, and yet they also appear to be deliberate. In all these ways they are comparable to, and preparations for, his final decision to retreat.

In another preparation for the retreat Rhisiart feels that Owen is 'a figure thus adorned and tended' who seems to have been 'prepared or had prepared himself for some mysterious sacrificial rite' (122), and later that there is something about Owen which 'approaches' 'a figure decked and adorned for sacrifice' (259). Owen takes the side of 'Sacrifice' in the opposition between 'the impulse to Power' and 'the impulse to Sacrifice' (W & S, 3) which has recurred in Powys's work since his first novel, *Wood and Stone*. Given he is aligned with sacrifice early on in the novel, it seems only right and proper that Owen's final act of rebellion should be to sacrifice his chance of making his signs of rebellion correspond to the realities of power, and instead leave us with the recognition that these signs are performatives.

There is an inescapable focus on the performative in *Owen Glendower*. This emphasis extends beyond the sense that utterances in the world of *Owen Glendower* are performatives to the sense that the utterance which consists of *Owen Glendower* is a performative. Powys develops our sense that *Owen Glendower* is performative when, for example, Owen rescues Rhisiart from Dinas Bran, and kills Fitz-Alan's Dorset soldier, Trenchard.

Trenchard dies in the arms of his friend, Tom Hardy, who is also from Dorset (380-1). In other words, Powys deliberately introduces into the world of *Owen Glendower* two minor characters, one of whom reminds us of the novelist Thomas Hardy, and the other of whom reminds us of a character in Hardy's novel *The Mayor of Casterbridge*, Michael Henchard. It is not possible for Thomas Hardy and a corrupted version his own fictional character to exist in the same world unless that world is fictional. It is not possible for either character to exist some 450 years before he was supposed to exist unless the world in which he exists is fictional. In other words, the main effect of Powys having characters who are suspiciously similar to Hardy and Henchard is to advertise the fictionality of his fictional world, to show us that it is a performative. As if having collected two characters from different worlds and set them down in his own fictional world is not a bold enough advertisement of the fictionality of his own fictional world, Powys advertises the advertisement as, in yet another reference to performance, he nicknames Trenchard 'Jimmy Mummer' (380).[16]

There are many other occasions on which Powys advertises the fact that the world of *Owen Glendower* is constructed by the words of *Owen Glendower*. Often he compares his own characters to characters in other fiction. Broch O' Meifod, for example, is big, strong and 'comical-looking', 'like a combination of the Show-Giant and the Show-Dwarf in Herefordshire Great Fair' (420), while Father Ignotus, the Archdeacon of Bangor, has 'the face of a mask in a morality play' (658). With characters like this around them, it is no wonder that Owen and Rhisiart both glimpse the performativity of the world they inhabit. As he waits for Owen to punish him, Rhisiart feels that he and all the other characters are '"parts of a – of a reality [...] that was like some timeless masquerade"' (660). When Owen encounters his eldest son and his bard, his first feeling is that 'they might well have been strolling actors in some English morality play' (472). The effect of these glimpses is to remind us that Rhisiart and Owen are right in their intuitions, that the world they inhabit is the equivalent of a masquerade, or a morality play, it is no more real, and just as performative.

At the end of the novel Powys uses an unrealistic device to free Tegolin for Rhisiart: Mad Huw dies of a fever from fishing in the Severn, and Dickon Shore dies of a surfeit of Severn fish (902). As well as making the device more obvious through its comic symmetry, Powys advertises it by referring to 'that providential catch of fish' (904). It is not simply that Powys is not attempting to hide his plot devices, or to hide the fact that his plots and his characters are performative, existing by virtue of his words. His techniques, such as descriptions of characters which emphasise their lack of realism, allusions to the fictionality of the world of the novel, and advertising of plot devices, are designed to show that his plots and his characters, his whole fictional world, is performative.

In Austin's terms, *Owen Glendower* emphasises its own performative illocutionary force, and de-emphasises its constative illocutionary force. We are to recognise, when reading the novel, that the words are constructing the facts we read about. Austin gives us a reason for saying that novels are performative utterances when he says that '"Hereby" is a useful criterion that the utterance is performative', and also that performatives may be performatives implicitly rather than explicitly (Austin, 57). If a novel was prefaced by 'Hereby', the entire novel would be regarded as a performative utterance. We would recognise that all the fictional world of the novel exists by virtue of all the words of the novel, in the same way that an apology exists by virtue of the word 'sorry'.[17]

Since performative utterances can be implicitly rather than explicitly performative, the word 'Hereby' is not necessary for the novel to be felt to have performative illocutionary force rather than constative illocutionary force. The feeling of performativity can be generated in other ways. In speech, the extent to which an utterance has implicit performative or implicit constative illocutionary force depends on factors such as tone of voice. In a novel, these factors are replaced by the novelist's technique, and so we can say that as a result of specific techniques, some relatively subtle, such as the advertising of the plot device of death by fishing and fish, some relatively obvious, such as the reference in *Wood and Stone* to 'The imaginary weaving of events, upon which we are just now engaged' (W & S, 8), Powys's novels are implicitly performative. Similar techniques are to be found in postmodernist works of art: one such is the device in film-making of letting the machinery of film-making appear on the screen.[18]

Four

Stella Gibbons's Parody of *Wolf Solent* in *Cold Comfort Farm*

In the third essay ("Peformativiy in *Owen Glendower*"), I said that Powys's techniques are designed to give his fiction performative illocutionary force. If Powys used different techniques, his fiction would have different illocutionary force. We can see this by comparing Powys's fictional version of Owen's rebellion to Lloyd's historical version. We might want to test the truth or falsity of Lloyd's history by checking its correspondence to 'how things really were', but to do the same for Powys's novel would be pointless. The reason for this is not simply that Lloyd's history is a history and Powys's novel is a novel, but that Powys employs many different techniques to draw attention to the performativity of his novel.[1]

In this essay I argue that Stella Gibbons's *Cold Comfort Farm* is a parody of Powys's novels,[2] and that the parody is the result of a difference of views between Gibbons and Powys as to what kind of utterance a novel should be. I have assumed that Gibbons thinks a novel should have constative illocutionary force, whereas Powys thinks a novel should have performative illocutionary force. These types of force are opposite categories. An utterance, or a novel, is a member of one category to the same extent as it is not a member of the other. The very techniques which increase an utterance's performative illocutionary force are the same techniques which reduce its constative illocutionary force. For example, it is not possible to say sorry in a way which is sarcastic and serious at the same time.

I have also assumed that Gibbons does not imagine that Powys's techniques are intended to make his novels performative. Instead, she judges his novels as if they were constatives, testing their correspondence to 'how (she thinks) things really are'. This is a rough test of correspondence, since novels are fictional, but it is a test which we make when we want to say whether or not a novel is realistic. Thus, it is not true that Holmes lived at 221b Baker Street, but it is true that someone like Holmes could have lived at some address like 221b Baker Street, so this aspect of the Holmes stories passes a rough test for correspondence to 'how (I think) things really are', and for me, this aspect of the Holmes stories is realistic.

Powys's novels are bound to fail this rough correspondence test, and it is this failure which prompts Gibbons's parody. Those of Powys's techniques which Gibbons parodies for their failure as constatives are just those techniques which are designed to show that his novels are performative. Gibbons parodies Powys's performatives (which, remember, she mistakes for constatives) by means of more performatives, so her novel advertises its own performativity in very similar ways to Powys's novel. The difference is that where Gibbons advertises performativity as a humorous method of parodying what she sees as failed constatives and contrasting them with her own (implicitly successful) constatives, what she sees as Powys's failed constatives actually advertise their own performativity as a serious method of showing the performativity of all utterances.

Gibbons indicates that *Cold Comfort Farm* is a parody when she says that it is 'meant to be... funny' (CCF, x). The first indication that Powys is being parodied comes in the dedication of the 'Foreword' to 'ANTHONY POOKWORTHY, ESQ.': the name contains all the letters of 'Powys' in the right order (CCF, ix). Gibbons indicates that she has taken Pookworthy as her model, and according to her descriptions, Pookworthy's books are very similar to Powys's. She tells Pookworthy, for example, 'Your books are more like thunderstorms than books' (CCF, xi). According to V.S. Pritchett in his 1929 review, *Wolf Solent* is 'as beautiful and strange as an electric storm'.[3] She asks, 'Shall I ever forget Mattie Elginbrod?' (CCF, xi). One of the characters in *Wolf Solent* is called Mattie Smith (127).[4]

Pookworthy's style is also very similar to Powys's. When reading Pookworthy, Gibbons is 'not always sure whether a sentence is Literature or where it is just sheer flapdoodle' (CCF, xi), and it is from Pookworthy that she learns that she must write 'as though I were not quite sure about what I meant but was jolly well going to say something all the same in sentences as long as possible' (CCF, x). Not only is Powys notable for long sentences, he is also noticeable for sentences in which he is not sure what he means, and sentences in which descriptive precision is sacrificed as lexical exhibitionism becomes an end in itself. These sentences are from *Wolf Solent*, but they could easily be by Pookworthy:

> Wolf felt his soul invaded by that peculiar kind of melancholy which emanates, at the end of a spring day, from all the elements of earth and water. It is a sadness unlike all others, and has perhaps some mysterious connexion with the swift, sudden recognition, by myriads

and myriads of growing things, of the strange fatality which pursues all earthly life, whether clothed in flesh or clothed in vegetable fibre. (104)

These sentences are Pookworthian in their use of subclauses which complicate rather than clarify, such as 'sudden', 'by myriads and myriads of growing things', and 'whether clothed in flesh or clothed in vegetable fibre'. They are also Pookworthian in their use of explicitly speculative terms such as 'perhaps'. Finally, they are Pookworthian in their use of imprecise, complex lexis. The 'melancholy' Powys describes becomes less clearly defined as he describes it. It is first defined only by its difference, as 'peculiar', then it is redefined as 'sadness'. The sadness is in turn defined first by its difference, as 'unlike all others', and then by reference to something else. It is connected, in a way which is itself 'mysterious', and the thing it is connected to is in turn not clearly defined. It is a 'recognition' by very many 'growing things' of a 'strange fatality', by which Powys could mean either 'death' or 'determinism'.

Gibbons tells us that she will put asterisks next to the 'finer passages', those passages which are 'Literature' (CCF, xi). This indicates that we should look to the asterisked passages for Pookworthian writing, and the first triple-asterisked passage in the novel (CCF, 48) is a clear imitation of Powys. Describing Adam Lambsbreath, Gibbons tells us

> From the stubborn interwoven strata of his subconscious, thought seeped up into his dim conscious; not as an integral part of that consciousness, but more as an impalpable emanation, a crepuscular addition, from the unsleeping life in the restless trees and fields surrounding him.

The Powysian elements here include the description of levels of consciousness, the qualification and vagueness, the use of the words 'strata' and 'emanation', and the interpenetration of man and nature. Powys describes Wolf's '"sinking into his soul"' in similar terms, telling us that it 'supplied him with the secret substratum of his whole life' (15), and that it ' consisted of a certain summoning-up, to the surface of his mind, of a subconscious magnetic power' (16). He also refers to the 'various layers' of Wolf's 'consciousness' (276). Urquhart refers to '"successive strata"' of '"human impression"' (41), and later we find out that 'The old rogue had discovered a completely new stratum of obscene Dorset legends' (295). He is qualified and vague when he describes Wolf's consciousness, saying, for example, that 'it would have been difficult to tell whether the goblinish grimaces that occasionally wrinkled his physiognomy were fits of sardonic chuckling or spasms of reckless desperation', and referring to 'His mood, whatever it may have been' (31). He also uses the term 'emanate' regularly (104, 146, 279, 324, 462, 510, 552), The interpenetration of man and nature is also important to Wolf, though he 'would never have confessed to any living person the intoxicating enlargement of personality that used to come to him from imagining himself a sort of demiurgic force, drawing to its power from the heart of Nature herself' (12).

Other asterisked passages of 'Literature' in *Cold Comfort Farm* imitate aspects of Powys's style. One double-asterisked passage contains a reference to '"all-forgiving and all-comprehending primeval slime"' (CCF, 76). In *Wolf Solent*, Powys refers to 'lakes of primal silence' (13) and to 'some primeval order of things, existing before good and evil appeared at all' (277), and tells us that Wolf's troubles are 'lost in the primal dew of the earth's first twilights' (407). In another double-asterisked passage Gibbons says

> After she had gone the hut sank into a dim trough of languor, pierced only by the shrill beam shed by the personality of Mrs. Beetle, which seemed to gather into one all the tenuous threads of the half-formulated desires of the two women which throbbed about them' (CCF, 85).

Here, Gibbons treats mental states as if they were physical entities, and Powys treats them in the same way. When Wolf is in the abbey at Ramsgard, Powys tells us that 'The high, cool, vaulted roof, with its famous fan-tracery, seemed to offer itself to his mind as if it were some "branch-charmed" vista of verdurous silence, along which his spirit might drift and float at large, a leaf among leaves!"' (28). Later, he tells us that 'What was left of consciousness within [Wolf] flapped like a tired bird against the whole dark rondure of the material universe' (569).

There are other stylistic imitations of Powys in *Cold Comfort Farm* apart from the asterisked passages. The names 'Starkadder', 'Lambsbreath' and 'Hawk-Monitor' repeat Powys's tendency to create names which are compounds, and names which include types of flora and fauna: the most similar example is 'Rook Ashover', from *Ducdame*. Both writers use archaisms: Gibbons has Adam refer repeatedly to Flora as '"Robert Poste's child"' (CCF, 62-65, 68-70), and Powys begins a paragraph with 'Ay' (18). Gibbons's Adam Lambsbreath uses the same stage rustic dialect as Powys's rustic characters. He worries about driving Flora back from the station, saying, '"'tes close on sixty-five years since I put hands to a pair of reins, and I might upset the maidy"' (CCF, 37). Torp tells Wolf '"Missus be cantiferous wi' I 'cos them 'taties be so terrible rotted"' (67). Powys uses ellipsis marks heavily in *Wolf Solent* to convey Wolf's train of thought (e.g. 15, 17, 295-6), and Gibbons imitates this technique in *Cold Comfort Farm* by using ellipsis marks to mark every possible shift of consciousness in her description of Ada Doom's train of thought (CCF, 140-4).

Gibbons also imitates Powys by using lists, referring, for example, to the 'dormers and mullions and scullions of Cold Comfort Farm' (CCF, 31). Wolf, imagining the world attacked by modernity and industry, sees it 'bleeding and victimized, like a smooth-bellied, vivisected frog [...] scooped and gouged and scraped and harrowed' (12). Here, Powys uses another characteristic stylistic device, a metaphor in which the vehicle complicates the definition of the tenor, rather than simplifying it. He uses this device again when he says that after Gerda stops imitating a blackbird, 'silence seemed to fall down upon that place like large grey feathers from some inaccessible height' (103). Gibbons imitates this technique too, when she refers to 'the solemn, tortured-snake voice of the sea [...] falling in sharp folds upon the mirror-expanses of the beach' (CCF, 32), and to Judith Starkadder's eyes as 'not eyes but voids sunk, between two jutting penthouses of bone and two jutting hummocks of cheek' (CCF, 261) (Wolf also has 'deeply-sunken grey eyes' [9], and John Malakite's eye sockets are 'hollow' [75] and 'sunken' [77]).

The aspects of Powys's style which Gibbons imitates in *Cold Comfort Farm* occur to roughly the same extent in all his novels written before 1932. I am focusing on *Wolf Solent* because in this case Gibbons appears to have imitated Powys's plot, as well as his style. Like *Wolf Solent*, Gibbons's novel begins with a train journey from a real London station (Waterloo in *Wolf Solent*, London Bridge in *Cold Comfort Farm*), to a fictional place in the country (Ramsgard, Howling) (9, CCF, 27). Both Wolf and Flora move from a realist world to a marvellous world to exploit family connections for financial support (10, CCF, 24). In both novels the marvellous world holds a secret which involves the protagonist, but which is never fully explained either to them or to us. Wolf travels to 'the very scene of [his] disturbing memories', to the place where his father fell 'by a series of mysterious headlong plunges, until he lay dead in the cemetery of that town, a byword of scandalous depravity' (10). When he arrives at the Otters' cottage, he thinks to himself, '"There's something funny about all this"' (37). Later he feels as if everyone he knows in Blacksod, Ramsgard and King's Barton is hiding from him something they know about Lenty Pond (344).[5] In *Cold Comfort Farm*, there are two unexplained secrets. Judith tells Flora, '"Child, my man once did your father a great wrong"' (22). We never discover what this wrong was, just as we never find out what it was Aunt Ada Doom saw in the woodshed (CCF, 296).

So far, we have seen how Gibbons imitates both Powys's style and Powys's plot. What we have yet to see is why we should see Gibbons's imitation as parodic. According to my initial assumptions, as well as creating a Powysian fictional world, Gibbons should include in her novel indications that this Powysian fiction world is a failed constative, that it does not correspond to 'how things really are', and she should do so by showing that it is a performative, in other words, not a world but a world version. This critical difference in Gibbons's novel is illustrated by the fact that though in both *Cold Comfort Farm* and *Wolf Solent*, the expectations of the protagonist are confirmed, the confirmation of expectations functions differently in each novel. At Barton Manor, Wolf's 'dream of the writing-table by a mullioned window "blushing with the blood of kings and queens"' turns out to be 'a literal presentiment' (57). This confirmation of expectations illustrates the fact that Wolf has moved from the realistic world of London to the marvellous world of King's Barton, without undermining the marvellous world. Later, Wolf says to himself, '"How unreal my life seems to be growing"' (181). In *Cold Comfort Farm*, the confirmation of expectations is more exact, and so more exaggerated, so as to make it clear not only that Flora moves from the realistic London world to the marvellous Howling world, but that the marvellous Howling world is simply a collection of 'Literary clichés'. Flora, for example, expects that Judith Starkadder will have a husband called Amos Starkadder and highly-sexed sons called Seth and Reuben (CCF, 18): this turns out to be the case (CCF, 38, 41). Later Gibbons makes it even clearer that Howling is a collection of clichés by pointing out the exact confirmation of expectations with the expression, 'of course'. At Cold Comfort, the hired girl is 'of course rather sullen-looking and like a ripe fruit' (CCF, 80). 'Of course, there were no preparations for tea in the kitchen', and there is 'no jam, of course' (CCF, 92).

So though both *Wolf Solent* and *Cold Comfort Farm* encourage us to see their marvellous worlds as to some extent constructed from the expectations of their protagonists, in *Wolf Solent* the resultant marvellous world is simply accepted (as I will argue, it is a world of the same order as the realist world, which competes on equal terms for Wolf's belief), whereas in *Cold Comfort Farm* the resultant marvellous world is shown to be a cliché. Powys's pluralism and Gibbons's parody also result in their protagonists having very different responses to these marvellous worlds. In *Wolf Solent*, Christie is described in terms which emphasise her marvellous qualities, as 'elfish', 'half-human', and a 'changeling' (221), as a 'slender young figure', a 'living, breathing plant', a 'passive entity', '"inhuman"' (twice), 'a young aspen tree', a 'mysterious girl', and an 'elfin creature' (247-54), as an 'Ariel', and an 'Elemental' (431), and as an 'evasive little being', a 'feminine Elemental', a 'sylph' and a 'nymph' (460). In *Cold Comfort Farm*, Elfine is described in similarly marvellous terms as a 'wild bird', a 'little flower' (CCF, 34), 'something like a kingfisher' (CCF, 45), as '"as wild and shy as a pharisee of the woods"' (CCF, 69).[6] But where, for Wolf, Christie seems to 'embody all his hovering, intangible dreams' (458), Flora decides that Elfine '"will have to be taken in hand at once"' (CCF, 71). For Wolf the confirmation of expectations in the marvellous world is positive, for Flora it is negative.

This different response to the marvellous world is also illustrated by the protagonists' different attitudes to aeroplanes. Aeroplanes appear at the beginning and end of both novels as the representatives of realism and the contemporary. In *Cold Comfort Farm* the aeroplane has positive connotations. Charles Fairford, the man Flora will marry, tells her before she goes to Howling, '"if you get very sick of it, wherever you are, 'phone me and I will come and rescue you in my 'plane."' (CCF, 11). He does come to collect her in his plane (CCF, 304-5), after she has corrected all the Starkadders' illusions and she phones him up to tell him '"there's nothing left for me to do here"' (299).

In *Wolf Solent*, aeroplanes have negative connotations. At the beginning of the novel, Powys tells us that Wolf

> felt as though, with aeroplanes spying down upon every retreat like ubiquitous vultures, with the lanes invaded by iron-clad motors like colossal beetles, with no sea, no lake, no river free from throbbing, thudding engines, the one thing most precious of all in the world was being steadily assassinated (12).

This precious thing is the ability 'to think any single thought that was leisurely and easy' (12). One of the leisurely, easy thoughts which Wolf is able to sustain in the marvellous world is the idea that Urquhart is his spiritual enemy, 'an antagonist who [embodies] a depth of actual evil' (44). For most of the novel Wolf is spared 'the atrocity of feeling the pinch of life's dilemmas against a background of monstrous modern inventions' (379), but immediately after he dismisses Urquhart's 'evil' as 'all gesture, all illusion' he hears the sound of an aeroplane, for the first time since he has arrived in Dorset (584-5).

In both *Cold Comfort Farm* and *Wolf Solent*, the arrival of the aeroplane at the end of the novel signals disillusionment, and the rejection of the marvellous world, in favour of the realist world. In *Wolf Solent*, it is Wolf who is disillusioned, and we are not encouraged to share his accept his rejection of the marvellous. Instead, both the realist and the marvellous worlds are seen as world versions, equally able to be labelled 'real'. This use of 'real' as a label begins early on in the novel, when Wolf applies it to the marvellous world, saying to himself, '"My life [...] hasn't been my real life at all! My 'mythology' has been my real life"' (17). If the label 'real' can be applied to both the world version in which Urquhart is Wolf's spiritual antagonist and the world version in which Urquhart is just a senile pervert (584), then this label cannot be thought of as referring to a correspondence between either world version and 'how things really are' (since the two versions are opposite, both cannot correspond to reality). So when Wolf describes his mythology as 'an escape from reality [...] that I was *bound* to lose, if reality got hold of me!"' (544), this indicates that Wolf has stopped believing in one world version and started believing in another world version, and has consequently shifted the label 'reality' onto the new world version.

As well as showing us that 'real' is a label which denotes Wolf's belief in a world version, rather than that world version's correspondence to 'how things really are', Powys also shows us that world versions are versions (in other words, performatives), rather than worlds (in other words, constatives), by showing them to be subjective and discursive. Wolf recognises that '"reality"' is a name which each person gives to their most significant experience (311-2), that there are various subjective realities, including 'the reality his mother lived in', and 'the reality Darnley lived in' (544). Though Jason Otter appears to see life stripped of its illusions (in much the same way as Flora does in *Cold Comfort Farm*), Wolf says '"what he sees when he's like is no less of an illusion than what I see when I'm plastered with armour"' (353). Wolf's final disillusionment, which occurs at the end of the novel, is presented as the acceptance of a new, discursive world version which he creates for himself through the figures of a field of buttercups (639-40), a cup of tea (644), and reference to Wordsworth (641).

As the shifts in the use of the label 'real' imply, Wolf is not disillusioned in the sense that his marvellous world version is displaced at the end of the novel by a realist world version which corresponds to how things really are. His disillusionment consists only in a change of mind, and Powys encourages us to think of it these terms by showing us his capacity to shift between marvellous and realist world versions early in the novel. In the space of two pages, Wolf begins to feel that 'he was probably exaggerating the peculiarities of King's Barton Manor', and decides, '"It's my nervous imagination, I expect"', and then asks himself, 'how far he really *had* exaggerated the sinister element in his employer's character' (122-3).

Although Wolf experiences the move from the marvellous world version to the realist world version as a move from illusion to disillusionment, the reader experiences it as a move from one performative to another. In *Cold Comfort Farm*, though, we are encouraged to see the marvellous world version as a failed constative, and the realist world version as a successful one. We reject the marvellous world version, firstly because Gibbons indicates that it is a parody, and secondly because Flora never believes in it. Her role is to correct the Starkadders' illusions rather than to become disillusioned herself. She is quite explicit about fulfilling this role when she tells Mrs. Smiling, '"When I have found a relative who is willing to have me, I shall take him or her in hand, and alter his or her character and mode of living to suit my own taste. Then, when it pleases me, I shall marry"' (CCF, 8). She does indeed alter the Starkadders' characters and modes of living, and the alteration consists of a move from unrealistic behaviour to realistic behaviour. At the end of the novel, she tells Charles, '"I've tidied everything up"' (CCF, 299).

Just as Flora tidies up the Starkadders, so Gibbons tidies up Powys. Flora draws attention both to the Starkadders' unrealistic behaviour, and to the fact that that behaviour is inappropriate. She does so, for example, when she tells Adam, '"I do feel that 'Robert Poste's child' every time is rather a mouthful, don't you think?"' (65). Gibbons imitations of Powys's style are similarly accompanied by critiques of that style, by some form of indication that the imitative passage is not a successful not a representation of 'how things really are'. One way in which she indicates this is by asterisking her passages of imitation to mark them as 'Literature'. Another is by following a passage of imitation with a piece of incongruous diction which gives the impression of undercutting vague Pookworthian fancy with hard realist fact. In the first triple-asterisked passage, for example, the description of Adam Lambsbreath's consciousness is undercut first by the everyday diction of the comment that the natural scene 'was more methodically arranged than you might think', and then by the everyday image of 'the vicar, driving home from tea at the Hall' (CCF, 49) which ends the paragraph. Similarly, as well as imitating Powys's characteristic device of the complicating vehicle, Gibbons critiques it. In *Wood and Stone*, Powys begins by telling us that Leo's Hill resembles 'a figure of a crouching lion' (W & S, 1). At the end of *Cold Comfort Farm*, when Flora has corrected the Starkadders' illusions, Gibbons tells us that 'The farmhouse itself no longer looked like a beast about to spring. (Not that it ever had, to her, for she was not in the habit of thinking that things looked exactly like other things which were as different from them in appearance as it was possible to be.)' (CCF, 266).

When Adam is waiting for Flora, Gibbons says that 'Humanity left him abruptly', and that 'If time passed (and presumably it did, for a train came in, and its passengers got out, and were driven away) there was no time for Adam' (CCF, 50). Here she is at once imitating and critiquing the Modernist theme of the subjectivity of time. This theme appears in the first paragraph of *Wolf Solent*, where Powys tells us that for Wolf, the three or four hour journey from Waterloo to Ramsgard lengthens itself 'into something beyond all human measurement' (9). This extension of time through subjectivity is repeated later in the novel (161), and Powys says that it seemed to Wolf that 'something in this Dorset air had the power to elongate the very substance of Time' (501).

The effect of Gibbons's parody is to reduce the world of *Cold Comfort Farm* to what is implicitly a successful constative. This reduction is achieved by parodying all those aspects of other fictional worlds which Gibbons sees as failed constatives, and showing them to be performatives, in other words, by showing them to be clichés of 'Literature'. Flora thinks that 'it was too true that life as she is lived had a way of being curiously different from life as described by novelists' (CCF, 105), and Gibbons indicates that her intention is to critique and correction this failed constativity by referring frequently to Jane Austen. Flora wants to write a novel like *Persuasion*, and thinks she has a lot in common with Austen (CCF, 14). Later she reads from *Mansfield Park* to refresh her spirits (CCF, 271). She and Gibbons do have a lot in common with Austen. They both set out to get rid of unrealistic generalisations and replace them with realistic ones. Austen does the same in *Emma*, where Emma's illusions are corrected just as the Starkadders' are corrected by Flora and in *Northanger Abbey*, where an unrealistic genre (Gothic) is parodied just as Powys's writing is parodied by Gibbons.

Flora sums up Gibbons's intentions when, describing some lingerie to Elfine, she tells her how 'all gross romanticism was purged away, or expressed only in a fold or a flute of material. She then showed how the same delicacy might be found in the style of Jane Austen, or a painting by Marie Laurencin' (CCF, 172). The problem with this purging in *Cold Comfort Farm* is that it requires the reader to accept Gibbons's version of 'how things really are', in other words, to accept as successful constatives those aspects of her novel which are not imitations and not critiques. Among the aspects of *Cold Comfort Farm* which I am personally disinclined to accept as successful constatives are the implicit racism of Gibbons's 'Jew-shop' (CCF, 14) and Mrs. Beetle's comment that the place is 'enough to choke a black' (CCF, 85), and the implicit homophobia of Mr. Mybug's comment that Mr.

Polswett is '"a bit homo, of course, but quite charming"' (CCF, 124).[7] Later, Mr. Mybug is the focus for more implicit racism, as Flora is depressed to find that his real name is Meyerburg, though her distaste for the Jewish name is such that she cannot learn to think of him as anything other than 'Mybug' (133-4, 151).

Cold Comfort Farm also requires us to accept Flora's snobbery as a successful constative when she thinks that

> One of the disadvantages of almost universal education was the fact that all kinds of persons acquired a familiarity with one's favourite writers. It gave one a curious feeling; it was like seeing a drunken stranger wrapped in one's dressing gown (CCF, 129).[8]

Flora's snobbery here also points to Gibbons's intentions for her novel. Though she makes fun of 'Literature' in her 'Foreword', the quarrel Flora has with Mr. Mybug, and by implication the quarrel Gibbons has with writers like Pookworthy (and Powys) is not that they are writing literature, but that they are using literature to say the wrong things, and to say them in the wrong way (in other words, they are using literature to write 'Literature'). Consequently Flora dismisses Mr. Mybug's reference to Shelley by comparing it to a one night stand, and Gibbons dismisses Pookworthy's (and Powys's) participation in literature by parodying it, so it no longer seems serious.

Cold Comfort Farm also requires us to accept particular forms of behaviour as 'natural'. We are told that 'Flora was pleased to see that the wild-bird-cum-dryad atmosphere which hung over Elfine like a pestilential vapour was wearing thin. She was talking quite naturally' (CCF, 160), and that 'When Flora planed away all the St. Francis-cum-barbola-work crust, she found beneath it an honest child, capable of loving calmly and deeply, friendly and sweet-tempered and fond of pretty things' (CCF, 171). Having been shown via parody that the Starkadder/ Powysian world is an illusion, an atmosphere, vapour or crust – is performative, we are to accept that the Flora/ Gibbons world, in which young girls talk, are friendly, are sweet-tempered and fond of pretty things, is constative. At Elfine's wedding, the Starkadders, their illusions now corrected by Flora, are seen, 'having a nice time. And having it in an ordinary human manner' (CCF, 284). By implication here, the Starkadders as they once were were not only extraordinary, but also inhuman.

It is just this reductive view of certain kinds of behaviour as ordinary and human, and certain types of utterance as corresponding to how things really are, which is challenged in *Wolf Solent*. Where Gibbons shows us that the Starkadders are wrong to believe in their world version because it is not reality and Flora is right to believe in hers because it is reality, Powys shows us that there are different realities for different people (as Wolf says, different realities for Wolf, his mother and Darnley), or, in Wolf's case, different realities for the same person. Powys's attitude is inclusive (where Gibbons's is exclusive) to the extent that he includes other world versions than Wolf's in the novel (where Flora simply corrects the illusions of the characters who disagree with her). When Gerda is concerned that she won't have anything to wear when Mrs. Solent comes to tea, and Wolf becomes 'suddenly aware of the existence, in the beautiful head opposite him, of a whole region of interests and values that had nothing to do with love-making and nothing to do with romance', he finds out that '"a girl's 'reality' is not my 'reality'!"' (232). It is this recognition that other people's world versions are different, rather than mistaken, which distinguishes Wolf, and *Wolf Solent*, from Flora and *Cold Comfort Farm*.

In this essay I have established a distinction between Powys's pluralist approach to the novel, an approach which treats the novel as a performative utterance, and Gibbons's dualist approach to the novel, an approach which treats the novel as a constative utterance (of more or less efficacy). This distinction, and in particular my contention that pluralists cannot parody, is significant for postmodernist fiction and theory, because postmodernism has been seen as typically parodic.

In 1982, for example, Blake Morrison referred to the 'fashionable postmodernist principle which decrees that the more parodistic a work of art is, the better'.[10] In her *Theory of Parody*, Linda Hutcheon quotes Morrison's equation of postmodernism and parody, and goes on to suggest that parody is 'a model of the prevailing norm', and to refer to parody's 'omnipresence today'.[11] Morrison, and more importantly Hutcheon, are clearly at odds with my conclusion that pluralism, and therefore postmodernism, cannot be parodic.

This difference of opinion would not matter if Hutcheon did not think postmodernism was pluralist, but she does: she says that 'In its absorption of conflicting codes, Post-Modernism is pluralistic and ironic' (Hutcheon, 114). Postmodernist art, however, and pluralist art in general, cannot be both pluralist and ironic (or parodic), since pluralism precludes irony (or parody). In parody, one world version is authorised as constative at the expense of another which is shown to be performative (for example, Flora's world version is authorised at the expense of the Starkadders, and Gibbons's world version is authorised at the expense of Powys's). In pluralist fiction all world versions are shown to be performative, so none can be authorised at the expense of the others.

It might be that Hutcheon is proposing a new theory of parody which dispenses with the idea that parody authorises one world version at the expense of another. She does say that what she is 'calling parody' 'is not just that ridiculing imitation mentioned in the standard dictionary definitions'. Instead, she defines parody as 'imitation characterized by ironic inversion', and later as 'repetition with critical difference' (Hutcheon, 5, 6, 20). However, her response to Woody Allen's *Play it Again Sam* illustrates the

extent to which her 'ironic inversion' and 'critical difference' do
constitute the authorisation of one world version at the expense of
another. She says of Allen's film

> the protagonist is not an antihero; he is a real hero, and his final sacrifice
> in the name of marriage and friendship is the modern and personal
> analogue to Rick's more political and public act. What is parodied is
> Hollywood's æsthetic tradition of allowing only a certain kind of
> mythologizing in film; what is satirized is our need for such
> heroicization. (Hutcheon, 25-26)

Hutcheon assumes that *Play it Again Sam* is a parody, and so she
is forced to look for something for it to ironise, to be 'critically
different' *from*. Since that something is clearly not the world
version in *Casablanca* itself (from the evidence of Allen's film, but
also because if it was, then Allen's film would be a parody
according to the straightforward dictionary definition), Hutcheon
invents a position for Hollywood and the general public to share,
and for Allen, as well as Hutcheon and us, since we are in on the
joke, to ironise and to be critically different from. The problem
with this is first of all it relies on a massive and unsupported
generalisation about the film industry and the public response to
it (it's the equivalent of saying that by imitating *The Odyssey*,
Joyce in *Ulysses* is parodying all the other works which have
imitated *The Odyssey* and accepted its position on the hero, and
satirising all those people who have believed that the only heroic
type of life is Odysseus's!), and secondly, that it does not really
alter our sense that parody is the authorisation of one world
version at the expense of another. It is just this kind of
authorisation which pluralism would disallow.

Notes

1   THE SATURNIAN QUEST IN *PORIUS*

1. G. Wilson Knight, *The Saturnian Quest: A Chart of the Prose Works of John Cowper Powys* (London: Methuen, 1964), 11, 19, 21.

2. In this essay, references to *Porius* are given in the text as page numbers only. References to Powys's other works are given with title abbreviations and page numbers.

3. The clearest statement I know is by Nelson Goodman, *Ways of Worldmaking* (Indianapolis: Hackett, 1978), 2-3, and for more general application to postmodernist theory, Steven Connor, *Postmodernist Culture: An Introduction to Theories of the Contemporary* (Oxford: Basil Blackwell, 1989).

4. Gilles Deleuze and Félix Guattari, *A Thousand Plateaus: Capitalism and Schizophrenia*, tr. Brian Massumi (London: Athlone Press, 1988), 238. Jean Baudrillard, *America*, tr. Chris Turner (London: Verso, 1988), 85.

5. William James, *Pragmatism*, ed. Bruce Kuklick (1907; Indianapolis: Hackett, 1981), 30. Richard Rorty, *Consequences of Pragmatism (Essays 1972-1980)* (Brighton: Harvester, 1982), xviii. Brian Massumi, Translator's Foreword: "Pleasures of Philosophy", *A Thousand Plateaus*, by Deleuze and Guattari, xiv. Gilles Deleuze, "Intellectuals and Power: Discussion with Michel Foucault", *Language, Counter-Memory, Practice*, by Foucault, tr. and ed. Donald Bouchard (Ithaca: Cornell University Press, 1977), 208.

6. William James, *Pragmatism*, *op. cit.*, 25. The problem is as follows. A man faces a tree. On the opposite side of the tree is a squirrel. The man walks round the tree, and as he does so the squirrel moves round the tree in the same direction, so the man never sees the squirrel. The man walks all the way round the tree until both man and squirrel are back in the

same position. The man has walked round the tree, but has he walked round the squirrel? World versions are the versions of the world produced by different frames of reference: see Goodman 2-3. For more on 'the supplement' see Jacques Derrida, *Of Grammatology*, tr. Gayatri Chakravorty Spivak (Baltimore: Johns Hopkins University Press, 1976), 157-9.

7. Foucault's opposition to subjectivity is typical of postmodernist theory. See Michel Foucault, *The Order of Things: An Archaeology of the Human Sciences*, [no translator given] (1970; London: Routledge, 1997), xviii, 387, and Michel Foucault, *The Archaeology of Knowledge*, tr. A. M. Sheridan Smith (1972; London: Routledge, 1997), 1.

8. Ferdinand de Saussure, *Course in General Linguistics*, tr. Roy Harris, ed. Charles Bally and Albert Sechehaye (London: Duckworth, 1983), 111. Saussure's assumption is wrong: see Steven Pinker, *The Language Instinct* (1994; London: Penguin, 1995).

9. Foucault's nominalism: *Archaeology*, 32 (on mental illness). See also Joseph Rouse, "Power/ Knowledge", *The Cambridge Companion to Foucault*, ed. Gary Gutting (Cambridge: Cambridge University Press, 1994), 93. Foucault on Borges: *Order*, xvi-xvii. See also Connor, 9.

10. For Paul De Man's nominalism see Jameson, 250.

11. Jacques Derrida, *Writing and Difference*, tr. Alan Bass (1978; London: Routledge, 1997), 54-55.

12. Jean Baudrillard, *Jean Baudrillard: Selected Writings*, ed. Mark Poster (Cambridge: Polity Press, 1998), 70, 89-90. Baudrillard is referring particularly to Roland Barthes, *S/Z*, tr. Richard Howard (New York: Hill and Wang-Farrar, Strauss and Giroux, 1974), 9.

13. Mark Poster, Introduction, *Jean Baudrillard: Selected Writings*, op. cit., 7.

14. Michel de Certeau, *The Practice of Everyday Life*, tr. Steven F. Randall (Berkeley: University of California Press, 1984), xxi. For comparison of Certeau and Baudrillard, see Poster, 7.

15. Ambivalence of symbolic exchange: Baudrillard, *Selected Writings*, 69. Loss of value for symbolic exchange: Baudrillard, *Selected Writings*, 124, for simulation: Jean Baudrillard, *The Transparency of Evil: Essays on Extreme Phenomena*, tr. James Benedict (London: Verso, 1993), 6. Baudrillard sees symbolic exchange and simulation as opposite rather than as analogous. See Connor 54-55, and Mike Gane, *Baudrillard: Critical and Fatal Theory* (London: Routledge, 1991), 11, 14.

16. Deleuze and Guattari, *Plateaus*, 137 (diagram of subjectivity deterritorialisation), 135 (diagram of deconstructive deterritorialisation), 134 (absolute deterritorialisation), 23 (abandonment of dualist correspondence between body, mind and language).

17. Foucault, *Order,* 34, 39-40. Baudrillard, *Selected Writings,* 150, 154. Gilles Deleuze and Felix Guattari, *Anti-Oedipus: Capitalism and Schizophrenia,* tr. Robert Hurley, Mark Seem, Helen R. Lane (London: Athlone Press, 1984), 180.

18. William James, "Does Consciousness Exist?" *Selected Writings,* ed. G. H. Bird (1904; London: Everyman-J. M. Dent, 1995), 101.

19. Deleuze and Guattari, *Plateaus,* 4 (books nonreferential), 5 (dialectical thought), 6-7 (rhizomes), 423 (nomadism). Foucault, *Archaeology,* 15. James, *Pragmatism,* 31.

20. Stanley Fish, "Commentary: The Young and the Restless", *The New Historicism,* ed. H. Aram Veeser (London: Routledge, 1989), 308. Jean Baudrillard, *The Illusion of the End,* tr. Chris Turner (Cambridge: Polity Press, 1994), 1.

21. Gianni Vattimo, *Beyond Interpretation: The Meaning of Hermeneutics for Philosophy,* tr. David Webb (Cambridge: Polity Press, 1997), 6-9.

22. Vattimo, *Beyond Interpretation,* 6-7, *The End of Modernity: Nihilism and Hermeneutics in Post-Modern Culture,* tr. Jon R. Snyder (Cambridge: Polity, 1988), 25.

23. Juliet Mitchell, "Femininity, Narrative and Psychoanalysis", *Modern Criticism and Theory: A Reader,* ed. David Lodge (Harlow: Longman, 1988), 428. Baudrillard, *Selected Writings,* 102. Robert Young, *White Mythologies: Writing History and the West* (London: Routledge, 1990), 1-6.

24. Massumi x, Michel Foucault, Preface, *Anti-Oedipus* by Deleuze and Guattari, xiii. Foucault says 'non-fascist' rather than 'anti-fascist' to avoid slipping from dehierarchisation to inversion.

25. Deleuze and Guattari, *Anti-Oedipus,* 131. Knight identifies the same theme in Powys (36).

26. Baudrillard, *Selected Writings,* 208. Deleuze and Guattari, *Plateaus,* 18-19.

27. For molar/ molecular see Deleuze and Guattari, *Plateaus,* 216.

28. Knight sees the Cimmerian and the Saturnian as equivalent (35).

29. Baudrillard's poetic style: Gane, 130. Deleuze and Guattari's deauthorisation: Foucault, Preface, xiv (see also Massumi, xiv). Deleuze and Guattari's literariness: Deleuze and Guattari, *Plateaus,* 4, flippancy: *Plateaus,* 22, 40-74.

30. Jean Baudrillard, *Simulacra and Simulation,* tr. Sheila Faria Glaser, *The Body, in Theory* (Ann Arbor: University of Michigan Press, 1994), 1.

31. Rhizomatic plot: Deleuze and Guattari, *Plateaus,* 8-9.

32. See Deleuze and Guattari on Professor Challenger, *Plateaus,* 49.

33. Deleuze and Guattari, *Anti-Oedipus,* 84, *Plateaus,* 482.

2   *PORIUS*, PLURALISM AND POWYS'S 'WEAK SENSE OF THE "OTHER"'

1. John Cowper Powys, *Porius: A Romance of the Dark Ages,* ed. Wilbur T. Albrecht (1951; Hamilton: Colgate University Press, 1994). References to *Porius* are given in the text as page numbers only. References to Powys other works are given with title abbreviations and page numbers.

2. Young, 2 (quoting Hélène Cixous on there being nothing to say about the other), 12 (dialogue in Levinas), 4 (dualism). Young is aware of the problems with the positions he articulates (6).

3. Emmanuel Levinas, "Is Ontology Fundamental?" *Basic Philosophical Writings*, ed. Adriaan T. Peperzak, Simon Critchley, Robert Bernasconi, Studies in Continental Thought (Bloomington and Indianapolis: Indiana University Press, 1996), 4, 5.

4. See Young, 15 for similarities and differences between Levinas and Derrida.

5. For translation and its relation to deconstruction see Valentine Cunningham on Emile Benveniste, in *In the Reading Gaol: Postmodernity, Texts, and History* (Oxford: Blackwell, 1994), 21-22.

6. Baudrillard, *Transparency*, 133.Young, 18.

7. Deleuze and Guattari, *Plateaus*, 188-9. Levinas 2 (subjectivity), 9-10.

8. Young, 15 (other calls into question the same). Levinas, 4-5.

9. James, *Pragmatism*, 30-31. Baudrillard is in a similarly anti-pluralist position when he says that it is the other which allows him not to repeat himself forever (*Transparency*, 174). How can this be if, as is the case under pluralism, when the other really is the other there is nothing to say?

10. Jeremy Hooker, "Romancing at the Cave-Fire: The Unabridged *Porius*", *The Powys Journal*, 4 (1994): 229.

11. Jon R. Snyder, Translator's Introduction, *The End of Modernity: Nihilism and Hermeneutics in Post-Modern Culture*, by Gianni Vattimo, tr. Snyder (Cambridge: Polity Press, 1988), xxii.

12. Homi K. Bhabha, "Minority Culture and Creative Anxiety", Conference Keynote, *Re-inventing Britain Conference*, The British Council (21.3.97); par. 14, online, WWW, 11 Sept. 1998.

13. Martin Buber, *I and Thou*, tr. Ronald Gregor Smith (Edinburgh: T. and T. Clark, 1944), 4.

14. Young , 14-15.

15. Mikhail Bakhtin, *Problems of Dostoevsky's Poetics*, trans., ed. Caryl Emerson, Theory and History of Literature., vol. 8 (Manchester: Manchester University Press, 1984), 185.

3   PERFORMATIVITY IN *OWEN GLENDOWER*

1. Judith Butler, *Gender Trouble* (London: Routledge-Routledge, Chapman and Hall, 1990), 25. Butler is not just talking about gender difference. For her, sex difference is not prediscursive either (148). Because Butler's assertions are so confident and have been so influential, it is worth repeating that all assertions that facts are discursive (or 'performatively constituted') are implicitly followed by the caveat, 'except the fact that all facts are discursive, which is nondiscursive'. If this seems abstract, consider the following, which makes the same attempt to reconcile anti-foundationalism with politics: 'Without the compulsory expectation that feminist actions must be instituted from some stable, unified, and agreed upon identity, those actions might well get a quicker start and seem more congenial to a number of "women" for whom the meaning of the category is permanently moot' (15). In attempting to avoid fixed categories, Butler ends up calling for political actions in which the actors don't know who or what the political action is for.

2. J.L. Austin, *How To Do Things With Words: The William James Lectures Delivered at Harvard University in 1955*, ed. J. O. Urmson and Marina Sbisà (1962; Oxford: Oxford University Press, 1975), 3, 5.

3. Jonathan Culler, *On Deconstruction: Theory and Criticism After Structuralism* (London: Routledge and Kegan Paul, 1983), 112-4.

4. Austin, 140 (truth via correspondence), 146 (constative and performative are abstraction and not expedient), 142-3 (overlapping of ways of appraising constative and performative), 143 (real life appraisals not simply true/ false tests), 143-4 (examples of real life utterances and how they are appraised).

5. Austin, 145 (rightness and properness dependent on the facts), 141 (example of batsman being out).

6. Jean Baudrillard, *The Transparency of Evil: Essays on Extreme Phenomena*, tr. James Benedict (London: Verso, 1993), 47.

7. Jean Baudrillard, *America*, tr. Chris Turner (London: Verso, 1988), 85.

8. Richard Palmer, "Toward a Postmodern Hermeneutic of Performance", *Performance in Postmodern Culture,* ed. Michel Benamou, Charles Caramello, *Theories of Contemporary Culture,* vol. 1 (Madison: Coda Press, 1977), 30.

9. Walter Scott, *Redgauntlet* (London: Macmillan, 1901), xxiii.

10. Jameson, 25. Michael Ondaatje, *In the Skin of a Lion* (1987; London: Picador, 1988).

11. Ian Duncan, 'The Mythology of Escape: *Owen Glendower* and the Failure of Historical Romance', *Powys Notes* (1992): 60.

12. R.R. Davies, *The Revolt of Owain Glyn Dwr* (Oxford: Oxford University Press, 1995), 226-7, 159, 90, 150-1. In this essay I use 'Owain Glyn Dwr' to refer to the real person, and 'Owen Glendower' to refer to Powys's character.

13. In this essay, references to *Owen Glendower* are given in the text as page numbers only. References to Powys's other works are given with title abbreviations and page numbers.

14. Campbell Tatham, "Mythotherapy and Postmodern Fictions: Magic is Afoot", *Performance in Postmodern Culture,* ed. Michel Benamou and Charles Caramello, Theories of Contemporary Culture, vol. 1 (Madison: Coda Press, 1977), 137.

15. James Hamilton Wylie, *History of England Under Henry the Fourth,* vol. 2 (London: Longmans, Green and Co., 1884), 302-3. J. E. Lloyd, *Owen Glendower: Owen Glyn Dwr* (Oxford: Clarendon Press, 1931), 104-5. In his 'Argument' Powys implicitly acknowledges that Wylie and Lloyd are his sources. For him, Wylie is 'Our best historian of Henry's reign', and Lloyd is 'The safest authority on the "documented" events of Owen Glyn Dwr's life' (940-1).

16. Powys is being rather disingenuous when he admits to having broken the proper rule of historical fiction by mentioning *Don Quixote* in his first paragraph (LNR 35 [6.3.41]), thus including in his novel references to things which did not exist until after the time of the novel (1400-1416). As the example of Hardy and Henchard shows, Powys goes on to disrupt our sense that Owen corresponds to a real situation which occurred between 1400 and 1416 in much more serious ways, indeed, these disruptions are an important aspect of his technique.

17. Austin is close to saying this when he includes the sub-heading '"A Novel"' in the list of speech devices, including 'Hereby', of which the performative is an example (73).

18. See Jean-François Lyotard, "The Unconscious as *Mise-en-Scène*", *Performance in Postmodern Culture,* ed. Michel Benamou and Charles Caramello, Theories of Contemporary Culture vol. 1 (Madison: Coda Press, 1977), 96.

4   STELLA GIBBONS'S PARODY OF *WOLF SOLENT* IN *COLD COMFORT FARM*

1. This has not stopped some critics criticising *Owen Glendower* for its historical inaccuracy: see Ian Duncan, *op. cit.,* 54-55, for a succinct summary of the different opinions on the novel.

2. According to her nephew and biographer, Reggie Oliver, the main targets of Gibbons's parody in *Cold Comfort Farm* are D.H. Lawrence and John Cowper Powys. Oliver provides evidence of Gibbons's antipathy to Powys's ideas by quoting from her unfavourable review of *In Defence of Sensuality*. Reggie Oliver, *Out of the Woodshed: The Life of Stella Gibbons* (London: Bloomsbury, 1998), 85-86. Since *Cold Comfort Farm* was published in 1932, the only Powys novels Gibbons can be parodying are *Wood and Stone, Rodmoor, Ducdame* and *Wolf Solent*. I think that plot similarities show that she is parodying *Wolf Solent* in particular, and I will focus on *Wolf Solent* in this essay. Gibbons is also parodying T.F. Powys. Flora's suggestion that Amos Starkadder go round the country in a Ford van, preaching on market days, alludes to *Mr. Weston's Good Wine*, which begins with a reference to Mr. Weston's Ford van. Stella Gibbons, *Cold Comfort Farm* (London: Longmans, Green and Co., 1932), 109 (further references to *Cold Comfort Farm* are given in the text with the abbreviation CCF). T.F. Powys, *Mr. Weston's Good Wine* (London: Chatto and Windus, 1927), 1.

3. V.S. Pritchett, "Below the Surface", *The Spectator,* 5276 (10.8.29): 198.

4. In this essay, references to *Wolf Solent* are given in the text as page numbers only. References to Powys's other works are given with title abbreviations and page numbers.

5. Powys uses this technique of creating an unexplained sense of foreboding as early as *Wood and Stone*, where Mrs. Fringe says to herself, '"if [only] the poor young man [Clavering] knew what this parish was really like"' (W & S, 160).

6. The extent to which Gibbons has a feel for Powys's style is demonstrated by the fact that while Elfine is not the name of any Powys character up until 1932, after *Cold Comfort Farm* was published, Powys wrote two novels in which Elphins do appear (*A Glastonbury Romance* and *Owen Glendower*).

7. Powys, of course, deals with homosexuality in *Wolf Solent* via Urquhart (27), and via Jason Otter and T.E. Valley (114), but his attitude is not derogatory. He does make jokes about it though: when Wolf asks if Mr. Urquhart is eccentric, '"queer, in fact"' Darnley says '"That depends [...] on what you mean by 'queer'"' (33).

8. Powys also comments on 'the universal spread of board-school education' in *Wood and Stone*. He considers its effect on local dialects, and says that it is because of universal education that the Andersens' girlfriends are 'expert bi-linguists', speaking 'the King's English' and 'Nevilton English' 'with equal ease' (W & S, 512). It is an indication of their differing social outlooks that while Powys considers the merits of universal education from the point of view of the working classes,

103

Gibbons considers its demerits from the point of view of the middle classes.

9. 'Pestilential vapour' alludes to Hamlet's 'foul and pestilent congregation of vapours'. William Shakespeare, *Hamlet, William Shakespeare: The Complete Works, Compact Edition,* general eds. Stanley Wells and Gary Taylor (Oxford: Clarendon Press, 1988), 666 (2.2.304-5). In *Wolf Solent,* Powys also alludes to this phrase, telling us that 'the sky was overcast with [...] a heavenly congregation of vapours' (149). Gibbons's Modernist and Powys's anti-realist sensibilities are demonstrated by their respective handling of the allusion. Where Gibbons alludes silently, Powys advertises the allusion with inverted commas, drawing attention to the construction of his fictional world. He also uses the allusion to convey the opposite sense to Hamlet's, demonstrating the multivalent significance of 'Literary' signs.

10. Blake Morrison, "The Pelvis on the Slab", *The Times Literary Supplement* (29.1.82), 111.

11. Linda Hutcheon, *A Theory of Parody: The Teachings of Twentieth-Century Art Forms* (New York: Methuen, 1985), 28, 29.

CRESCENT MOON PUBLISHING

ARTS, PAINTING, SCULPTURE

The Art of Andy Goldsworthy: Complete Works(Pbk)
The Art of Andy Goldsworthy: Complete Works (Hbk)
Andy Goldsworthy in Close-Up (Pbk)
Andy Goldsworthy in Close-Up (Hbk)
Land Art: A Complete Guide
Richard Long: The Art of Walking
The Art of Richard Long: Complete Works (Pbk)
The Art of Richard Long: Complete Works (Hbk)
Richard Long in Close-Up
Land Art In the UK
Land Art in Close-Up
Installation Art in Close-Up
Minimal Art and Artists In the 1960s and After
Colourfield Painting
Land Art DVD, TV documentary
Andy Goldsworthy DVD, TV documentary
The Erotic Object: Sexuality in Sculpture From Prehistory to the Present Day
Sex in Art: Pornography and Pleasure in Painting and Sculpture
Postwar Art
Sacred Gardens: The Garden in Myth, Religion and Art
Glorification: Religious Abstraction in Renaissance and 20th Century Art
Early Netherlandish Painting
Leonardo da Vinci
Piero della Francesca
Giovanni Bellini
Fra Angelico: Art and Religion in the Renaissance
Mark Rothko: The Art of Transcendence
Frank Stella: American Abstract Artist
Jasper Johns: Painting By Numbers
Brice Marden
Alison Wilding: The Embrace of Sculpture
Vincent van Gogh: Visionary Landscapes
Eric Gill: Nuptials of God
Constantin Brancusi: Sculpting the Essence of Things
Max Beckmann
Egon Schiele: Sex and Death In Purple Stockings
Delizioso Fotografico Fervore: Works In Process 1
Sacro Cuore: Works In Process 2
The Light Eternal: J.M.W. Turner
The Madonna Glorified: Karen Arthurs

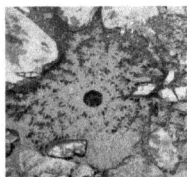

LITERATURE

J.R.R. Tolkien: The Books, The Films, The Whole Cultural Phenomenon
Harry Potter
Sexing Hardy: Thomas Hardy and Feminism
Thomas Hardy's *Tess of the d'Urbervilles*
Thomas Hardy's *Jude the Obscure*
Thomas Hardy: The Tragic Novels
Love and Tragedy: Thomas Hardy
The Poetry of Landscape in Hardy
Wessex Revisited: Thomas Hardy and John Cowper Powys
Wolfgang Iser: Essays
Petrarch, Dante and the Troubadours
Maurice Sendak and the Art of Children's Book Illustration
Andrea Dworkin
Cixous, Irigaray, Kristeva: The *Jouissance* of French Feminism
Julia Kristeva: Art, Love, Melancholy, Philosophy, Semiotics and Psychoanalysis
Hélène Cixous I Love You: The *Jouissance* of Writing
Luce Irigaray: Lips, Kissing, and the Politics of Sexual Difference
Peter Redgrove: Here Comes the Flood
Peter Redgrove: Sex-Magic-Poetry-Cornwall
Lawrence Durrell: Between Love and Death, East and West
Love, Culture & Poetry: Lawrence Durrell
Cavafy: Anatomy of a Soul
German Romantic Poetry: Goethe, Novalis, Heine, Hölderlin, Schlegel, Schiller
Feminism and Shakespeare
Shakespeare: Selected Sonnets
Shakespeare: Love, Poetry & Magic
The Passion of D.H. Lawrence
D.H. Lawrence: Symbolic Landscapes
D.H. Lawrence: Infinite Sensual Violence
Rimbaud: Arthur Rimbaud and the Magic of Poetry
The Ecstasies of John Cowper Powys
Sensualism and Mythology: The Wessex Novels of John Cowper Powys
Amorous Life: John Cowper Powys and the Manifestation of Affectivity (H.W. Fawkner)
Postmodern Powys: New Essays on John Cowper Powys (Joe Boulter)
Rethinking Powys: Critical Essays on John Cowper Powys
Paul Bowles & Bernardo Bertolucci
Rainer Maria Rilke
In the Dim Void: Samuel Beckett
Samuel Beckett Goes into the Silence
André Gide: Fiction and Fervour
Jackie Collins and the Blockbuster Novel
Blinded By Her Light: The Love-Poetry of Robert Graves
The Passion of Colours: Travels In Mediterranean Lands
Poetic Forms
The Dolphin-Boy

POETRY

The Best of Peter Redgrove's Poetry
Peter Redgrove: Here Comes The Flood
Peter Redgrove: Sex-Magic-Poetry-Cornwall
Ursula Le Guin: Walking In Cornwall
Dante: Selections From the Vita Nuova
Petrarch, Dante and the Troubadours
William Shakespeare: Selected Sonnets
Blinded By Her Light: The Love-Poetry of Robert Graves
Emily Dickinson: Selected Poems
Emily Brontë: Poems
Thomas Hardy: Selected Poems
Percy Bysshe Shelley: Poems
John Keats: Selected Poems
D.H. Lawrence: Selected Poems
Edmund Spenser: Poems
John Donne: Poems
Henry Vaughan: Poems
Sir Thomas Wyatt: Poems
Robert Herrick: Selected Poems
Rilke: Space, Essence and Angels in the Poetry of Rainer Maria Rilke
Rainer Maria Rilke: Selected Poems
Friedrich Hölderlin: Selected Poems
Arseny Tarkovsky: Selected Poems
Arthur Rimbaud: Selected Poems
Arthur Rimbaud: A Season in Hell
Arthur Rimbaud and the Magic of Poetry
D.J. Enright: By-Blows
Jeremy Reed: Brigitte's Blue Heart
Jeremy Reed: Claudia Schiffer's Red Shoes
Gorgeous Little Orpheus
Radiance: New Poems
Crescent Moon Book of Nature Poetry
Crescent Moon Book of Love Poetry
Crescent Moon Book of Mystical Poetry
Crescent Moon Book of Elizabethan Love Poetry
Crescent Moon Book of Metaphysical Poetry
Crescent Moon Book of Romantic Poetry
Pagan America: New American Poetry

MEDIA, CINEMA, FEMINISM and CULTURAL STUDIES

J.R.R. Tolkien: The Books, The Films, The Whole Cultural Phenomenon
Harry Potter
Cixous, Irigaray, Kristeva: The *Jouissance* of French Feminism
Julia Kristeva: Art, Love, Melancholy, Philosophy, Semiotics and   Psychoanalysis
Luce Irigaray: Lips, Kissing, and the Politics of Sexual Difference
Hélene Cixous I Love You: The *Jouissance* of Writing
Andrea Dworkin
'Cosmo Woman': The World of Women's Magazines
Women in Pop Music
Discovering the Goddess (Geoffrey Ashe)
The Poetry of Cinema
The Sacred Cinema of Andrei Tarkovsky (Pbk and Hbk)
Paul Bowles & Bernardo Bertolucci
Media Hell: Radio, TV and the Press
An Open Letter to the BBC
Detonation Britain: Nuclear War in the UK
Feminism and Shakespeare
Wild Zones: Pornography, Art and Feminism
Sex in Art: Pornography and Pleasure in Painting and Sculpture
Sexing Hardy: Thomas Hardy and Feminism

In my view *The Light Eternal* is among the very best of all the material I read on Turner. (Douglas Graham, director of the Turner Museum, Denver, Colorado)

The Light Eternal is a model monograph, an exemplary job. The subject matter of the book is beautifully organised and dead on beam. (Lawrence Durrell)

It is amazing for me to see my work treated with such passion and respect. (Andrea Dworkin)

Sex-Magic-Poetry-Cornwall is a very rich essay... It is like a brightly-lighted box. (Peter Redgrove)

CRESCENT MOON PUBLISHING
P.O. Box 393, Maidstone, Kent, ME14 5XU, United Kingdom.
01622-729593 (UK) 01144-1622-729593 (US) 0044-1622-729593 (other territories)
cresmopub@yahoo.co.uk   www.crescentmoon.org.uk

www.ingramcontent.com/pod-product-compliance
Lightning Source LLC
Chambersburg PA
CBHW062001040426
42447CB00010B/1860